Happy Cooking.
Happy Birthday
lots of love

Joan Richard
+ Hannah xxx

PASTA
COOKBOOK

PASTA
COOKBOOK

More than 150 international
recipes for starters, soups, sauces,
casseroles and main dishes, with special
step-by-step instructions on creating
homemade pasta

Ⓜ

MEREHURST PRESS
— LONDON —

Published 1990 Merehurst Limited
Ferry House
51/57 Lacy Road
Putney
London
SW15 1PR

Copyright © 1989, 1990 Ottenheimer Publishers, Inc.
This 1990 edition published by Ottenheimer Publishers, Inc.,
for Merehurst Limited under the Merehurst Limited imprint.

Published originally under the title Nudeln,
by Gräfe und Unzer GmbH, München
Copyright © 1988 Gräfe und Unzer GmbH, München

English translation copyright © 1988 by Ottenheimer
Publishers, Inc.

Text by Annette Wolter
Photographs by Odette Teubner

Printed in Hong Kong

ISBN: 1-85391-122-4

Contents

About this Book

Here's everything you ever wanted to know about pasta. The recipes are simple and easy to follow and the full colour photographs are sure to inspire you to sample some of the delicious dishes.

Pasta comes in all shapes and sizes, from large sheets of lasagne to tiny stars and shells for soups. Learn how to make the most of this nutritious food and discover some of the delicious ways it can be cooked and served.

Pasta dishes can be filling and satisfying or can be light and delicate. In this book you'll find recipes for every occasion, whether it's a simple starter, an elegant dinner or a hearty supper for the family.

Italy is today the indisputable home of pasta and consequently all the famous Italian dishes are to be found in this comprehensive collection, such as *Lasagne al Forno* (page 88), *Spaghetti Bolognaise* (page 50) and *Spaghetti con Aglio e Olio* (page 30). However, as well as the famous dishes, look out too for some of the many less known but still delicious regional specialities, like *Genoese Vegetable Soup* (page 17) and *Tagliatelle with Tomatoes, Mushrooms and Sage* (page 34).

As well as giving you the chance to sample some of the huge variety of Italian pasta dishes, this book also contains pasta recipes from other parts of the world such as Austria, Germany and Switzerland. From China, Japan and Korea there are a whole host of delicious dishes to tempt and delight your family and friends, from delicious *Crispy Wontons* (page 40) to complete meals like oriental *Noodles with Horseradish* (page 72) or *Chow Mein* (page 73).

Homemade pasta is in a class of its own, yet it is not difficult to make, even without a pasta machine. In Chapter 1, step-by-step recipes show you how to create your own pasta, illustrating not only how easy it can be, but also how you can make pasta really your own by adding your own favourite flavouring and colouring.

To enjoy pasta at its best, cook it only until 'al dente'. Follow the guide for cooking pasta on page . . . and you can't go wrong!

Types of Pasta

Spaghetti—This is the best known pasta and comes in long straight strands of varying thickness that go under such names as *spaghettini, vermicelli* and *capellini*. To cook spaghetti, place the ends in a pan of boiling water and then gently coil it into the pan, pushing down as it softens in the boiling water. To eat spaghetti, twirl it into a spoon, using a fork.

Macaroni—a thicker, hollow tube, sold either in long lengths, like spaghetti, or cut into short lengths. *Canneloni*, large thick tubes of pasta, *penne, zite* and the ribbed *rigatoni* all go under the general heading of macaroni, as does *elbow macaroni*, short curved pieces of hollow pasta.

Lasagne—These large sheets of pasta are most commonly used to make the dish of the same name, which traditionally is made with a Bolognaise sauce. As well as plain lasagne, look out for *lasagne verdi* (coloured green with spinach) and wholewheat lasagne, made with wholewheat flour.

Tagliatelle—Commonly referred to simply as noodles or in Rome as *fettucini,* this ribbon shaped pasta is sold either in nests or in loose coils. Fresh, shop bought tagliatelle is widely available nowadays in most supermarkets.

Pasta Shapes—Shells, bows, wheels and twists are just some of the huge variety of pasta shapes available in shops. The medium-sized shapes can be used in all sorts of made up dishes or served with sauces. The tiny shapes, which also include stars, "rice grains," hoops and butterflies are known as soup pasta and are added to anything from a hearty minestrone to a light clear consommé.

Stuffed Pasta—*Tortellini* and *ravioli* are the most famous of the stuffed pastas. Small bite-sized envelopes of pasta are stuffed with fillings that include chopped chicken, veal, ham, pork, cheese, nuts, spinach, Swiss chard or any tender vegetable.

Gnocchi—Though not strictly pasta, gnocchi is eaten in Italy in the same way as pasta and commonly goes under the same heading. There are several varieties, the most common ones being made from ricotta cheese and spinach, mashed potato or semolina. They are normally cooked in boiling water and are ready when they rise to the surface.

Chinese noodles—Whether the Chinese introduced pasta to Italy or vice versa, Chinese noodles are clearly the eastern equivalent of Italian tagliatelle. They are made principally from wheat flour, rice flour or pea starch and come in a variety of thicknesses. They can be boiled or deep fried.

Wontons—Similar to Italian *ravioli*, these little packages of pasta enclose delicately flavoured meat, fish and/or vegetable fillings. Wonton wrappers can be homemade or bought frozen from Chinese supermarkets.

The Value of Pasta

Translated literally, pasta is Italian for dough and it's not surprising therefore that the term encompasses so many different types, shapes and sizes of food. The Italians are easily the greatest consumers of pasta, and in the south, where the essential hard wheat grows, pasta is a staple food. However, while Italy is thought of as the home of pasta, it is by no means its only habitat. Austria and Germany have a wide variety of speciality 'nudels' and dumpling dishes, while China and the Far East have been serving noodles for literally centuries.

In Italy, there are said to be over 500 different varieties of pasta, the Italians having a penchant for bizarre and amusing shapes which they like to add to their soups or top with sauces. Tiny pasta car radiators, racing cars, flying saucers, letters and numerals are just a few that can be found in shops throughout Italy, and although only a mere 50 or so are available in this country, one can be forgiven for having difficulty remembering all the various types, especially since so many go by different names according to which particular region they come from. Don't, however, be daunted by such confusion. Most pastas are interchangeable, providing they are basically the same shape. If the recipe says twists, and you can only get shells or bows, then buy what you fancy. Pasta is not a food with hard and fast rules.

There are basically two types of pasta; pasta made simply from flour and water and egg pasta *(pasta all'uovo)* which, by law, if made commercially, must contain five eggs per kilo of flour. Both are available dried but fresh pasta is normally the *Pasta all'uovo* variety. Coloured pasta is made by adding purées of vegetables to the dough.

However, while spinach and tomato are the most commonly used vegetables for colouring pasta commercially, there's no reason why beetroot, carrots or red peppers, all suitably cooked

and puréed, shouldn't be kneaded into a homemade pasta dough.

There was once a time when pasta, along with bread and potatoes, was considered horribly fattening and a definite "no-no" for anyone on a calorie-controlled diet. Thankfully for all pasta lovers, the tables have been turned. Pasta is now appreciated for what it is—a nutritious, healthy and wholesome food. It is an excellent source of carbohydrate, the most important and best "energy" food, and it's not surpising that athletes, especially long distance runners who need to build up large reserves of energy, consume great quantities of pasta in the weeks and days before a race. (At London's Marathon, the organizers arrange pasta parties for all contestants the evening before the race.) Pasta is also low in fat, high in protein, magnesium, phosphorous, zinc and several B vitamins. Of course, it will be fattening if the other ingredients in the dish are high in calories. However, if served with high protein, low calorie foods like

chicken, or with vegetables and low-fat cheeses, pasta can easily be incorporated into a calorie controlled diet. Many of the recipes in the chapter on Pasta Salads are low in calories. If in doubt, reduce or cut out the dressing.

Pasta made with wholewheat flour has a pleasant, slightly nutty flavour and a more chewy texture. Since it has a stronger taste, it is best served with a strongly flavoured sauce. Like wholemeal bread, it contains more vitamins and minerals than normal pasta and has as much as five times more fibre. You will find it takes slightly longer to cook and since it is naturally chewy, cook it until it is fairly tender.

Dried pasta is widely available in all shapes and sizes (see opposite). The best pasta is made from durum wheat *(semola di grano duro)* and tagliatelle and lasagne are now widely available made with eggs, either plain, coloured or wholewheat. Plain pasta should be clear yellow/cream, without any greyish tinge. If possible, look out for pasta made in southern Italy, especially the Abruzzi. Fresh pasta, mainly tagliatelle, spaghetti, ravioli and tortellini, can now be brought from most supermarkets—look in the chilled food containers

and check the sell-by date, since fresh pasta only has a limited shelf life.

Contrary to popular belief, dried pasta won't keep indefinitely. It is best used within 6-8 months after purchase and once opened should be used within 2 months. Store it in a dry cool place and, if coloured, preferably in the dark, since it will fade if kept in a sunny position. Fresh pasta should be stored in the refrigerator and used within 2 days since it will begin to dry out after that. If you don't need it immediately, it will freeze successfully for up to 3 months.

In Italy, homemade pasta is made with hard durum semolina flour. However, since this is virtually unobtainable in this country, unless you're lucky enough to live near a good Italian delicatessen, the next best thing is plain strong white flour. Plain flour can also be used, although it cannot be rolled out as thinly by hand and is best used only when you have a pasta machine. If adding oil to the dough, use olive oil for a distinctive and authentic flavour. Sunflower oil also gives good results but avoid blended vegetable oils or frying oils as they often have an overpowering flavour. For wholewheat pasta, use either strong plain wholewheat flour or half and half wholewheat and strong plain white flour which gives a lighter result.

Homemade Pasta

To Make the Dough

Pasta is made from plain flour, eggs, some oil and salt and is unbelievably simple if you just give yourself a little time and observe a few basic rules. For 4 people you will need 225–350 g/8–12 oz (2–3 cups) plain strong white flour, 2–3 eggs, a little salt and 2-3 tsp. oil. Fresh eggs give the dough a better flavour and preferably all ingredients should be about the same temperature. Once you have made the pasta it can be cut into flat noodles or other shapes and should then be laid out on a floured tea-towel to dry.

Sift the flour onto a work surface; make a hollow and add the eggs, oil and salt. Working outward from the middle, use the fingers of one hand to mix the flour into the egg mixture, at the same time using the other hand to cup the rim of flour and prevent the eggs from moving out.

Machine Made Pasta

Kneading and rolling—the hardest part of pasta making—becomes a thing of the past if you use a pasta-making machine. These simple hand operated machines are available from any kitchen shop and have a variety of attachments for making spaghetti, lasagne or even filling and cutting ravioli. Although "connoisseurs" will have you believe "handmade" pasta is best, for the rest of us, the difference is barely distinguishable—yet the time and effort saved is enormous. Dough made in a pasta machine needs no resting before shaping.

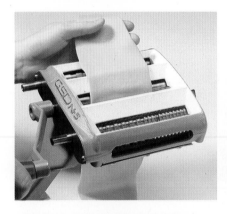

Make up the dough and knead by hand until it is no longer sticky. Open the machine as wide as possible and turn the lightly floured dough, in batches, through the machine. Repeatedly gather up the dough and turn it through the machine until it shines and becomes as wide as the roller.

Colouring Pasta

Pasta can be coloured in a variety of ways. This not only makes it look spectacular, but also adds a subtle flavour. Blanched spinach, either finely chopped or puréed, gives green pasta, while chopped fresh herbs give an attractive speckled appearance. For orange pasta add cooked puréed tomatoes or tomato purée (paste), and for startling crimson, add puréed beetroot. Because most of these ingredients contain liquid, add a little more flour while kneading and rolling out.

Blanch the spinach, rinse in cold water and drain thoroughly. Purée and combine with flour, eggs, oil and salt. If using a pasta machine, cooked spinach can be simply finely chopped.

Cooking Pasta

There is one basic rule to cooking pasta—**don't overcook it**. To check, remove a little from the pan with a fork; it should no longer be hard or taste of flour, but should still have a firm centre and be elastic. This is known as "al dente"—"firm to the bite." Pasta is best freshly cooked, drained and then mixed with a vegetable or meat sauce and, if desired, a sprinkling of cheese.

To cook 400 g/14 oz pasta, bring 4 litres/8 pts water to the boil, and add 2 tsp salt and 1 tbsp oil. The oil will prevent the pasta from sticking to itself or the bottom of the pan and will also help prevent the pan from boiling over. Gradually ease the pasta into the boiling water.

Knead the dough, backwards and forwards, with the palm of the hand, pressing it flat, folding, and then flattening again, until the dough is shiny and pliable. This will take 10–15 minutes. If the dough becomes too firm, knead in a few drops of water. Leave the dough to rest for 1 hour under an inverted bowl.

Roll out the dough as thinly as possible on a floured work surface (2-3 mm/¹⁄₁₀th-¹⁄₈th in thick for stuffed pasta). For ribbons or other shapes, cut out using a pasta cutting wheel or a sharp knife. A ruler will help give you a straight edge. With stuffed pasta, continue working immediately, but allow unfilled pasta to dry briefly before cooking.

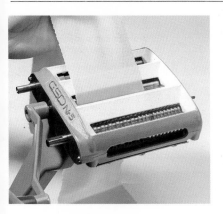

When ready to shape the pasta, gradually reduce the setting on the machine until you obtain the desired thickness. Take care to keep the dough stretched out to its full length making sure it does not fold back on itself. It should glide out onto the work surface like a ribbon.

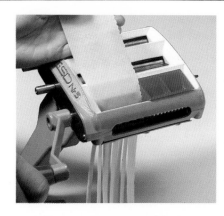

Fit the required attachment and cut the pasta to the required shape. Tagliatelle, flat noodles and spaghetti should then be left to dry for about 30 minutes before cooking. They can be placed on a floured tea towel, or, if very long, draped over the arm or back of a chair.

For orange pasta, cook tomatoes and purée to a thick paste. Add a few finely chopped herbs and 1 tbsp tomato purée (paste). Combine with flour, eggs, oil and salt. Knead dough and roll out as above.

Cook a medium-sized beetroot until tender (about 45–90 minutes). Peel, chop and purée and knead into the pasta with the other ingredients. Make sure beetroot is completely cold before adding.

Stir pasta once or twice with a wooden spoon and then cook, uncovered, in fast boiling water. Cooking time for dried pasta depends on size. Spaghetti, tagliatelle and large pasta take 8–10 minutes; small shapes 2–8 minutes; lasagne about 12 minutes. Check packet instructions. Fresh pasta takes about 3 minutes.

Pour the pasta into a colander and drain thoroughly. For salads or made-up dishes, rinse it in cold water to prevent it from overcooking. If serving warm, however, dot with butter and mix with sauce immediately or keep warm, covered, in a warm oven until ready to use. Remember, however, not to keep pasta waiting for too long!

Homemade Pasta

Homemade Tortellini

Today you can buy tortellini from almost any good supermarket or delicatessen. However, homemade tortellini, stuffed with tasty fillings like prawns, meats, cheese or vegetables is far superior to anything you can buy and is also far easier to make than you'd think. The fillings can be as varied as you wish. Blend them with puréed vegetables, cheese and herbs for a variety of flavours.

Mix together minced beef, finely chopped onion, salami, grated cheese and 1 egg yolk. Roll out dough to 3 mm/⅛th in thickness and cut into 4 cm/1½ in rounds. (Cover any dough that is not immediately being used with a damp cloth.) Place 1 tsp of filling just off centre of the circles.

To Prepare Lasagne

You don't have to be an expert cook to make a great lasagne, although it does take a little time. Homemade lasagne is excellent. Cook for 2-3 minutes in boiling water before assembling the dish. The no-cook shop-bought lasagne needs no pre-cooking, but normal dried lasagne should be boiled before being assembled. Read instructions on packet for timings. A Bolognaise sauce generally is used in lasagne. It should be simmered until well thickened. Make lots of white bechamel sauce and, if possible, use fresh Parmesan cheese which you can grate yourself at home.

Butter a shallow oblong ovenproof dish and add a layer of Bolognaise sauce. Spread a layer of bechamel sauce over and top with sheets of lasagne.

Bolognaise Sauce

Bolognaise meat sauce is probably the best known of all the sauces to serve with pasta. As well as the favourite sauce with lasagne, it is also excellent with spaghetti and could be used as the basis for many other pasta meals. This recipe, originating as you'd expect from Bologna, is considered to be the original recipe. It takes a bit of time, so make a large quantity and freeze what isn't immediately required.

Gently fry 100 g/4 oz lean streaky bacon in 2 tablespoons olive oil; add 1 diced onion, carrot, celery stick and garlic clove and cook until softened. Add 400 g/14 oz minced beef and fry, stirring, until meat loses its pink colour and becomes brown.

Pesto Sauce

Pesto is a simple uncooked sauce, based principally on fresh basil which is puréed to a paste. Other ingredients include garlic, pine nuts, olive oil and freshly grated Parmesan cheese. It is delicious with all kinds of freshly cooked, preferably homemade pasta. In Genoa it is stirred into minestrone soup by the spoonful. Whenever fresh basil is available, it's well worth the effort to make a good supply of pesto and freeze it in small portions. It makes a wonderful surprise on cold winter days.

Crush 2 finely chopped cloves garlic with 1 heaped tablespoon lightly toasted pine nuts in a mortar. Then add a good handful washed and dried basil leaves and pound in the same way.

Brush the edges with water. Fold the circles over and press together firmly. Carefully shape the semi-circles into a crescent with the tip of the forefinger, and press the ends together.

Cook the tortellini 8–10 minutes in rapidly boiling salted water. Drain well. Drizzle the pasta with melted butter, and sprinkle with browned bread-crumbs. Serve the tortellini with a complementary sauce.

Place a second layer of minced meat sauce and bechamel sauce on top, and cover with the last sheets. Spread bechamel sauce over the pasta sheets, so that no corners of the dough stick out, otherwise the uncovered corners will dry out while baking.

To finish the lasagne, sprinkle generously with freshly grated Parmesan cheese, and finally with breadcrumbs. Tiny cubes of Mozzarella or flakes of butter may also be sprinkled on top.

Pour in 125 ml/4 fl oz/½ cup red wine and cook uncovered until liquid evaporates. Add 250 ml/8 fl oz hot/1 cup meat stock and 400 g/14 oz peeled finely chopped tomatoes. Crush the tomatoes with the cooking spoon.

Season the Bolognaise sauce with freshly chopped parsley, dried oregano, tomato purée, salt and pepper and cook for 1 hour over a low heat. Partially cover the pan, and occasionally stir the sauce.

Transfer the purée into a bowl. Stirring constantly, add 1 tablespoon grated cheese and a few drops of olive oil. Alternatively, use an electric whisk to blend together, or make entirely using a food processor.

Add 75 g/3 oz/¾ cup freshly grated Parmesan and some 5 tablespoons olive oil. Season the pesto with salt and freshly ground black pepper, cover and leave to stand for at least 1 hour. Before serving mix 2 tablespoons of the pasta cooking water into the pesto.

Pasta Soups
and Starters

Herb Soup with Pasta

Quick and inexpensive

Cooking time: 30 minutes
Serves 4

½ head lettuce
½ bunch each chives, dill, and parsley
2 sprigs basil
1 litre/2 pt/4 cups chicken stock (instant)
100 g/4 oz vermicelli
100 g/4 oz/¾ cup frozen peas
1 tsp butter
Pinch each salt and white pepper
Pinch grated nutmeg
4 egg yolks

Break the lettuce into leaves, wash, dry and cut into strips. Wash the herbs and pat dry. Chop the chives, dill and parsley finely, and pluck the small leaves off the basil. • Bring the chicken stock to the boil, and add the pasta and peas. Let the soup cook, partially covered, over a moderate heat for 4 minutes. Add the finely chopped herbs, the lettuce strips, and the butter to the soup, and heat briefly. Season with salt, pepper and nutmeg. Gently slide 1 egg yolk into each soup plate or cup, pour the soup over, and sprinkle basil over. Serve at once.

Austrian Mushroom Soup

Easy and economical

Drying time: 1 day
Preparation time: 40 minutes
Cooking time: 5 minutes
Serves 4

For the dough:
100 g/4 oz/1 cup strong plain white flour
Pinch of salt
1 egg
For the soup:
1 tbsp sunflower oil
1 litre/2 pt/4 cups hot vegetable stock
1 tbsp dried mushrooms
Pinch each salt and grated nutmeg
1 egg yolk
½ bunch parsley

Sift the flour onto a board, make a hollow in the middle, add the egg and salt, and knead to a firm, smooth dough; gradually add a little more flour. Rub the dough through a medium-sized grater, and spread the "pearls" out to dry on a tea towel overnight. • The next day, heat the oil in a saucepan. Brown the "pasta pearls" until golden, stirring. Pour the vegetable stock over and bring to the boil. Wash the dried mushrooms thoroughly in a sieve, and add them to the soup. Cook for 5 minutes. • Season the soup with nutmeg and salt, and remove from the heat. Blend the egg yolk with 1 tbsp of hot soup, and stir into the soup. • Wash the parsley, pat dry, chop finely and sprinkle over the soup.

Tip: The dough needs to be firm for grating. It is a good idea to put it in the freezer for 15 minutes

before grating. Well-dried "pasta pearls" can be stored in a tightly sealed jar for up to one month.

Tagliatelle and Chickpea Soup

Inexpensive but takes time

Preparation time: 12 hours (including soaking peas)
Cooking time: 1 hour 40 minutes
Serves 4

250 g/9 oz/1¼ cups chickpeas
½ tsp salt
2 sprigs rosemary
3 garlic cloves
75 g/3 oz streaky bacon
1 litre/2 pt/4 cups (approx.) clear beef stock
150 g/5 oz tagliatelle
Pinch each salt and white pepper
4 tbsp grated Parmesan cheese

Cover the chickpeas with cold water and leave to soak for 12 hours. • Drain, cover with fresh water and bring to the boil. • Wash the rosemary. Peel the garlic cloves. Simmer the chickpeas, covered, with 1 garlic clove and 1 sprig of rosemary over a moderate heat for about 1½ hours. • Chop the bacon, the leaves from the remaining sprig of rosemary and the garlic very fine. • Strain the cooked chickpeas, reserving the cooking liquid. Cover the chickpeas and keep warm. Discard the rosemary sprig and garlic clove. • Add the cooking liquid to the meat stock to make up to 1.5 litres/3 pt/6 cups, and bring to the boil once more. Stir the chopped rosemary, garlic cloves and bacon into the soup, add the tagliatelle and cook until just tender, but not too soft. • Season the soup with salt and pepper and reheat the chickpeas in the soup; do not

allow the soup to come to the boil again. Serve with grated Parmesan.

Pasta Soup with Basil

Easy and tasty

Preparation time: 45 minutes
Serves 4

350 g/12 oz potatoes
1.5 litres/3 pt/6 cups vegetable stock (instant)
2 ripe beef tomatoes
150 g/5 oz spaghetti
1 bunch basil
½ tbsp olive oil (virgin oil)
Pinch each salt and white pepper
2 tbsp grated Parmesan cheese

Wash and peel the potatoes, rinse again, cut into cubes and simmer in the vegetable stock for about 15 minutes. • Skin the tomatoes by plunging into boiling water. Chop roughly; add to the soup and cook for an additional 10 minutes. • Break the spaghetti into pieces, place in the soup until just cooked but not too soft— about 5 minutes. • Wash the basil and pat dry. Strip the leaves from the stem and chop. • Stir the oil into the soup, and season. • Turn the soup into 4 soup bowls, each garnished with basil and ½ tbsp Parmesan cheese.

Sauerkraut Soup

Main meal recipe

Preparation time: 30 minutes
Serves 4-6

2 onions
1 sprig each parsley, tarragon and chervil
2 tbsp sunflower oil
1 tbsp plain wholewheat flour
500 g/18 oz sauerkraut
1.25 litres/2½ pt/5 cups vegetable stock
1 bay leaf
150 g/5 oz/1 cup small pasta shells
4 small spicy sausages
1 tsp freshly chopped parsley
1–2 pinches ground black pepper
½ tsp paprika

Peel and chop the onions finely. Wash the herbs and chop finely. • Heat the oil in a large pan, and sauté the onion and the herbs. Add the wholewheat flour and cook, stirring, for 1 minute. Chop the sauerkraut, and add it to the onion mixture. Add the bay leaf. Cover and cook over low heat for 15 minutes. • Bring the salted water to the boil and cook the pasta for about 10 minutes. Add pasta and stock to the soup. • Cut the sausages into slices and mix into the soup. Discard the bay leaf. Stir in the parsley, and season the soup with the pepper and paprika to taste.

Peasant Soup

Simple and nourishing

Preparation time: 15 minutes
Cooking time: 10 minutes
Serves 4

1.25 litres/2½ pt/5 cups vegetable stock
2 tsp chopped parsley
300 g/11 oz potatoes
150 g/5 oz/1 cup garden peas
150 g/5 oz/1 cup green or wholewheat pasta spirals
½ bunch dill
1 tbsp soured cream
½ tbsp butter
1 pinch white pepper

Bring the vegetable stock and parsley to the boil. • Meanwhile, peel, wash, and chop the potatoes, and add them to the boiling stock with the peas and pasta. Cook together 10 minutes. • Wash the dill, pat dry and chop the leaves finely, discarding the stem. Remove the pan from heat. Mix the soured cream, butter and chopped dill into the soup and season to taste with pepper and a little salt if necessary.

Tip: If required, the soup may be made even more substantial by scattering 100 g/4 oz of crisply grilled, chopped bacon over the portions. Chervil may be substituted for dill. With fresh fruit for dessert, this makes a "quick" menu.

Genoese Vegetable Soup

An Italian speciality

Preparation time: 80 minutes
Serves 6

2 onions
225 g/8 oz courgettes (zucchini)
100 g/4 oz carrots
150 g/5 oz green beans
2 tbsp olive oil
1.5 litres/3 pt/6 cups hot vegetable stock
Pinch each salt and freshly ground black pepper
3 garlic cloves
200 g/7 oz/1½ cups rosmarini (rice shaped pasta)
½ bunch each basil and parsley
1 tbsp grated Parmesan cheese

Peel the onions and chop finely. Wash, top and tail the courgettes. Scrape the carrots under running water and chop. Also dice the courgettes (zucchini). Wash the beans and cut into small pieces. • Heat the olive oil in a saucepan. Fry the chopped onions until transparent, add the chopped vegetables and fry for 10 minutes, stirring often. • Pour the vegetable stock over, cook the soup for 15 minutes, and season to taste. • Peel the garlic cloves, chop very finely, and cook with the soup for a short while. • Add the pasta and cook for a few minutes until 'al dente'. • Wash the herbs, pat dry, and strip off the leaves from the stems before chopping the leaves. Serve the soup garnished with herbs and cheese.

Pasta Soup with Savoy Cabbage

Inexpensive and easy

Preparation time: 1 hour
Serves 6

½ head Savoy cabbage, approx. 600 g/1 lb
1 onion
½ tbsp olive oil
Pinch freshly grated nutmeg
1.5 litres/3 pt/6 cups hot beef stock
150 g/5 oz/2 cups pasta shells
1 bunch parsley
Pinch each salt and freshly ground black pepper
1 tbsp grated Pecorino or Parmesan cheese

Discard the outer leaves from the Savoy cabbage, cut through the half, and discard the hard stalk. Shred the quarters of cabbage finely, rinse in cold water and drain well. Peel the onion and cut into thin rings. • Heat the oil, and fry the onion rings until transparent. Add the shredded cabbage and cook approx. 10 minutes, stirring occasionally. • Season the cabbage with the nutmeg, and pour the beef stock over. Cook in a covered pan over a low heat for 30 minutes. • Add the pasta shells and cook until 'al dente'. • Wash the parsley, pat dry, discard the stems and chop the leaves finely. • Season the soup with salt and pepper to taste, and serve with grated cheese and parsley.

Beef and Bean Soup with Pasta

Very tasty

Preparation time: 2½ hours
Serves 8

2.5 litres/5 pt/10 cups water
1 tsp salt
1 kg/2¼ lb shin of beef, sliced
Beef bones for stock
1 onion
1 bouquet garni
500 g/18 oz French beans
200 g/7 oz vermicelli
1 garlic clove
½ bunch each chives and parsley
Pinch black pepper

Bring the salted water to the boil. • Wash the meat and bones. Peel the onion and add it with the bouquet garni, meat, and bones to the boiling water. Simmer the meat gently for 2 hours; during the first 15 minutes remove the scum from the surface. • Trim the beans, wash, cut into pieces and cook covered in salted water for 10 minutes. Cook the pasta in salted water for about 4 minutes, drain and leave to cool in colander. • Peel the garlic and chop finely. • Remove the bones from the stock, and carefully discard the fat and sinews, chopping the remaining meat carefully. Strain the stock. • Wash the herbs, pat dry and chop finely. Add the beans, the meat, the garlic and the vermicelli to the stock. Season and sprinkle with herbs.

Neapolitan Pasta Soup

An Italian speciality

Soaking time: 12 hours
Preparation time: 20 minutes
Cooking time: about 1 hour
Serves 4

100 g/4 oz/⅔ cup butter (lima) beans
1 litre/2 pt/4 cups vegetable stock
1 bouquet garni
100 g/4 oz wholewheat tagliatelle
1 tsp salt
500 g/18 oz tomatoes
1 garlic clove
6 tbsp olive oil
2 tsp chopped fresh or ½ tsp dried oregano
Pinch cayenne pepper

Leave the beans to soak in 1 litre/2 pt cold water overnight. • Drain the beans through a colander and place in the vegetable stock with the bouquet garni. Simmer for about 45 minutes in a covered pan. Discard bouquet garni. • Cook the noodles in fast boiling salted water for about 7 minutes until 'al dente', then strain, rinse in cold water and set aside. Dip the tomatoes briefly into boiling water, peel, discard the stalky part, and chop the flesh. • Peel and finely chop the garlic, and fry in the oil until transparent. Add the chopped tomatoes, oregano and cayenne pepper, and cook, stirring, for 5 minutes, then stir with the noodles into the bean soup. • Reheat the soup briefly, and season to taste.

Tomato Soup with Cheese Gnocchi

A delicious meal in itself

Preparation time: 40 minutes
Serves 4

For the soup:
2 ripe beefsteak tomatoes
40 g/1½ oz butter
1 tsp wholemeal flour
1 litre/2 pt/4 cups hot vegetable stock
Pinch each salt and white pepper
2 sprigs thyme
1 sprig rosemary
For the dumplings:
2 hard-boiled eggs
1 egg
2 tbsp cottage cheese, strained
3 tbsp wholemeal flour
Pinch each salt and grated nutmeg

Make a cross in the skin of the bottom of the tomatoes with the point of a knife, and immerse briefly in boiling water. Remove skin and stalky part in middle. Chop the flesh. • Melt 25 g/1 oz butter, and fry the flour until golden. Stir in the chopped tomatoes, and pour in the vegetable stock. Season with salt, pepper, leaves of thyme and rosemary, and cook for 10 minutes. • To make the dumplings, shell the hardboiled eggs, chop, and mash with a fork. Add the remaining butter, the egg, the cottage cheese and the flour and mix to a smooth, pliable but firm dough. Season with salt and nutmeg. • Dip a teaspoon in hot water and use to shape the dumplings. Let the dumplings cook in the soup until they rise to the surface; the soup should only be simmering gently.

Pea Soup with Herby Gnocchi

Easy and inexpensive

Preparation time: 15 minutes
Cooking time: 20 minutes
Serves 4

2 leeks
100 g/4 oz carrots
1 tbsp cooking oil
200 g/7 oz/1½ cups frozen peas
1 litre/2 pt/4 cups hot chicken stock
1 egg
50 g/2 oz soft butter
150 g/5 oz/1¼ cups plain flour
½ tsp dried mixed herbs
Pinch salt and paprika
10 small leaves peppermint

Remove the dark green tops of leaves and the root ends from the leeks. Cut leeks in half lengthwise, wash thoroughly and cut into fine strips. Scrape and wash the carrots, cut lengthwise and then cut into small strips. • Heat the oil in a saucepan and stir fry the vegetable strips with the peas; add the chicken stock, and cook for 15 minutes. • To make the gnocchi, mix the egg and butter well with a fork. Add the flour and dried herbs, and knead to a pliable dough. • Dip a teaspoon into the boiling soup and use it to shape the gnocchi. Let the gnocchi cook in the soup until they rise to the surface. Season the pea soup with salt and paprika. • Wash the mint leaves, chop finely and use to garnish.

Siberian Pasta Shells

Worth the effort

Preparation time: 45 minutes
Resting time: 1 hour
Cooking time: 10–15 minutes
Serves 4

300 g/11 oz/2¾ cups strong plain white flour	
2 eggs	
½ tsp salt	
1 small onion	
250 g/9 oz minced beef	
½ tsp salt	
Pinch white pepper	
1 egg yolk	
1 litre/2 pt/4 cups beef stock (home-made or instant)	
½ bunch dill	

Mix the flour with the eggs, salt and as much lukewarm water as necessary to make a firm but pliable pasta dough. • Peel the onions, chop very finely and mix into the minced beef with the salt and pepper. • Roll the dough out to ⅛ in/3 mm thickness on a lightly floured surface and cut out circles about 1½ in/4 cm in diameter. Paint the edges with lightly beaten egg yolk. • Divide the minced meat stuffing among the pieces of dough, fold each piece in half and press the edges together with a fork. Leave stuffed pasta shapes to rest for 1 hour. • Bring the beef stock to the boil, and simmer the pasta shapes for about 10–15 minutes. • Wash and chop the dill and use to garnish before serving.

Stuffed Pasta Triangles

Intricate and attractive

Preparation time: 40 minutes
Resting time: 1 hour
Cooking time: 10 minutes
Serves 4

2 eggs	
½ tsp salt	
1 tbsp oil	
150–200 g/5–7 oz/1¼–1¾ cups strong plain white flour	
225 g/8 oz cooked chicken	
2 tbsp chopped parsley	
1 small onion	
25 g/1 oz butter	
½ tsp salt	
Pinch each black pepper and ground ginger	
1 litre/2 pt/4 cups chicken stock	

Mix the eggs with the salt and oil. Gradually add the sifted flour, to make a firm dough. • Mince the chicken as finely as possible, and add 1 tbsp parsley to it. Peel the onion, chop finely and add to the meat with the butter, salt, pepper and the ginger. • Roll out the dough to ⅛ in/3 mm thick and cut into squares of approx. 2 in/5 cm. Divide the stuffing among the squares. Fold each square in half diagonally, and use a fork to crimp the edges together firmly. Leave the stuffed pasta shapes to dry on a floured tea towel for 1 hour. • Bring the chicken stock to the boil, and gently cook the pasta shapes for 10 minutes. • Serve the soup garnished with the remaining parsley.

Pasta Soup with Tomatoes

Simple and tasty

Preparation time: 40 minutes
Serves 4

4 large ripe tomatoes
1 litre/2 pt/4 cups water
2 vegetable stock cubes
1 tsp oil
100 g/4 oz vermicelli
3 eggs
2 tsp lemon juice
2 tbsp chopped fresh herbs, e.g. chives, basil or parsley

Make a cross in the skin at the bottom of each tomato with a sharp knife, cover with boiling water, and leave for a few minutes. • Bring the water to the boil and dissolve the stock cubes. • Remove the tomato skins, chop the flesh into chunks, and discard the stalky centre. Strain or liquidise the tomato flesh, and add to the stock with the oil. Bring the soup back to the boil. Drop in the vermicelli and cook until 'al dente'—about 4 minutes. • Take the soup off the heat and keep warm, covered. • Separate the eggs. Beat the egg whites with lemon juice until stiff. Blend in the yolks one at a time into the whites with an egg whisk. • Gradually stir 8 tbsp of hot soup into the egg mixture. Then blend the egg mixture into the remaining soup. • Garnish the soup with herbs and serve.

Winter Vegetable Soup with Pasta

Nourishing

Preparation time: 30 minutes
Cooking time: 25 minutes
Serves 4

1 small swede (400 g/14 oz)
¼ celeriac (200 g/7 oz)
2 carrots (200 g/7 oz)
¼ white cabbage
1 large onion
1 tbsp oil
1 litre/2 pt/4 cups hot beef stock
100 g/4 oz vermicelli
1 tbsp chopped fresh parsley

Wash the swede, celeriac, and carrots under running cold water, peel or scrape, rinse again and slice thickly. Remove the outside leaves from the white cabbage, cut out and discard the centre core, wash and shred. Peel and chop the onion. • Heat the oil in a large pan, and fry the onions until transparent, stirring constantly. Add the remaining vegetables, briefly turning them in the oil, and pour the beef stock over. Cook the vegetables, covered, for about 20 minutes. • Add the vermicelli, stir the soup thoroughly and cook for about 4 minutes, until the pasta is 'al dente'. Serve garnished with chopped parsley.

Tip: The soup tastes even better when served with 1 tbsp of soured cream to each portion.

Pasta Soup with Borlotti Beans

A classic Italian soup

Soaking time: 12 hours
Preparation time: 15 minutes
Serves 4

225 g/8 oz/1 cup dried borlotti beans
1 small onion
2 garlic cloves
75 g/3 oz lean streaky bacon
250 g/9 oz ripe tomatoes
1 bunch parsley
4 tbsp olive oil
Approx. 1 litre/2 pt/4 cups meat stock
1 tsp mixed dried herbs
Pinch of black pepper
150 g/5 oz/1 cup short cut macaroni
2 tbsp grated Parmesan cheese

Soak the beans in water overnight. • Drain, cover with fresh water and cook for approx. 1 hour until tender, then drain in colander reserving the cooking liquid. Meanwhile, peel the onion and garlic and chop finely. Chop the bacon, peel the tomatoes and cut into pieces. Wash and pat dry the parsley, and chop finely. • Heat the oil in a sufficiently large saucepan, and cook the onion and garlic until transparent. Add the bacon, parsley, tomatoes and beans, and simmer, covered, for about 20 minutes. Strain or liquidise half of the mixture. • Pour the reserved bean cooking liquid onto the unstrained vegetables and add the meat stock. • Continue cooking the soup: season with mixed dried herbs and pepper. Cook the macaroni in the soup until 'al dente' and whisk the vegetable purée into the soup. Heat the soup thoroughly and sprinkle with grated cheese before serving.

Potato and Pasta Soup

Inexpensive and easy

Preparation time: 45 minutes
Serves 4-6

1 onion
100 g/4 oz lean streaky bacon
250 g/9 oz waxy potatoes
25 g/1 oz butter
1.5 litres/3 pt/6 cups beef stock
Pinch each salt and white pepper
200 g/7 oz/1½ cups macaroni
2 tbsp chopped fresh parsley

Peel the onions and chop into small cubes. Likewise, dice the bacon. Wash, peel and rinse the potatoes and cut into paper thin slices. • Heat the butter in a saucepan and fry the bacon and onions, stirring constantly for 10 minutes until golden. • Pour the beef stock over, and season with salt and pepper. Bring to the boil, then add the sliced potatoes, and cook for 10 minutes. Add the pasta to the pan, stir well and cook uncovered until the pasta is just cooked, but not too soft. Sprinkle the parsley over the soup before serving.

Tip: 1 or 2 garlic cloves can be substituted for the onion and, to save calories, 200 g/7 oz mushrooms for the bacon.

Pasta and Courgette (Zucchini) Soup

Simple and inexpensive

Preparation time: 1 hour
Serves 4-6

1 onion
500 g/18 oz small courgettes (zucchini)
2 large ripe tomatoes
4 tbsp olive oil
1.5 litres/3 pt/6 cups hot beef stock
150 g/5 oz/1 cup macaroni
½ bunch each basil and parsley
Pinch each salt and freshly ground black pepper
2 tbsp grated Parmesan

Peel and chop the onion finely. Wash, dry, top, tail and chop the courgettes (zucchini). Plunge the tomatoes into boiling water, peel, cut into pieces and discard the stalky centre. • Heat the oil in a large pan. Fry the onion until transparent, add the chopped courgettes (zucchini) and tomatoes and sauté, stirring constantly. Pour the beef stock over and bring to the boil. Add the pasta, stir once and cook for 6 minutes until 'al dente'. Wash and pat dry the herbs, and chop the leaves finely. Stir into the soup and season with salt and pepper. Before serving add grated cheese.

Soup with Homemade Pasta

A meal in itself

Preparation time: 50 minutes
Serves 4

50 g/2 oz/½ cup each plain flour and soy flour
1 tsp mixed dried herbs
½ tsp vegetable purée (paste)
½ tsp ground cumin
1 small egg
1 tbsp sesame seed oil
250 g/9 oz new potatoes
150 g/5 oz carrots
50 g/2 oz butter
150 g/5 oz/1 cup shelled green peas
200 g/7 oz iceberg lettuce
1 litre/2 pt/4 cups vegetable stock
Pinch each salt and pepper
2 tbsp chopped fresh parsley

To make the dough, combine the flours with the dried herbs, vegetable purée (paste) and cumin, and mix to a firm but pliable dough with the egg and the oil. Shape into a roll and leave to rest beneath an inverted dish for 30 minutes. • Scrape the potatoes, scrape the carrots, wash and chop. Wash the lettuce, cut into quarters and then cut each quarter into 2–3 pieces. Fry the potato and carrot in butter with the peas for 2–3 minutes. Add the lettuce and vegetable stock. Cook for about 10 minutes, then season with salt and pepper. • For the pasta, bring salted water to the boil. Grate the dough on a coarse grater, and bring the pieces of dough to the boiling point. Strain the dough pieces through a sieve, and add to the soup with the parsley.

Turkey and Pasta Soup

Nourishing

Preparation time: 1¾ hours
Serves 4-6

2 turkey wings (approx. 800 g/1¾ lb)
1.5 litres/3 pt/6 cups water
1 tsp salt
1 bay leaf
5 white peppercorns
1 tsp dried mixed herbs
150 g/5 oz each carrots, broccoli, leeks and mushrooms
50 g/2 oz butter
150 g/5 oz/2 cups wholemeal pasta shapes
2 tsp herb seasoning
2 tbsp chopped fresh parsley

Wash the turkey wings and cook with salt, bay leaf, peppercorns and dried herbs in water for 45 minutes. • Trim and wash the vegetables. Chop the carrots and break up the broccoli coarsely. Cut the leeks into rings and slice the mushrooms. • Remove the turkey wings from the stock, discard skin and bones, and chop the flesh into chunks. Strain the stock. • Heat the butter in a pan and fry the vegetables for 1–2 minutes, stirring frequently. • Add the pasta shapes to the soup, stir and cook for 8–10 minutes. • Add the meat and season the soup with the herb seasoning. • Garnish with parsley before serving.

Beef Pasta Casserole

A main meal soup

Preparation time: 1 hour
Serves 4

250 g/9 oz green peppers
500 g/18 oz tomatoes
250 g/9 oz topside of beef
Pinch freshly ground black pepper
2 onions
2 garlic cloves
5 tbsp olive oil
1 litre/2 pt/4 cups vegetable stock
1 bunch mixed fresh herbs
1 tsp each paprika and ground cumin
½ tsp dried thyme
100 g/4 oz/2 cups wholemeal pasta spirals
2 pinches chilli powder
1 tbsp each chopped fresh parsley and chives
100 g/4 oz Mozzarella

Quarter the green peppers, wash, discard seeds and pith, and cut into narrow strips. Peel the tomatoes and chop the flesh. Chop the meat and season with the pepper. • Peel and chop the onions and garlic, fry in olive oil and remove with a slotted spoon. Brown the meat in two batches in the oil, then add the onions, garlic and previously prepared vegetables and fry briefly. Put the vegetable stock, herbs, paprika, cumin and thyme into the pan, and cook all together for 15 minutes, covered. • Place the pasta in the soup, and cook for about 8 minutes, uncovered. • Stir in the chilli, parsley and chives. Do not allow the soup to cook any longer. Grate the cheese finely and sprinkle over the soup.

Wonton Soup

Tricky but worth the effort

Preparation time: 1¾ hours
Serves 6

200 g/7 oz/1¾ cups flour
1 egg
125 ml/4 fl oz/½ cup water
1 tsp salt
2 spring onions
100 g/4 oz canned bamboo shoots
100 g/4 oz chopped pork
100 g/4 oz chicken breast fillets
1 tbsp each soy sauce and sake (rice wine)
Pinch each salt and white pepper
1 egg white
3 litres/6 pt/12 cups water
2 tsp salt
1 litre/2 pt/4 cups chicken stock
1 handful each mustard and cress

Sift the flour into a bowl. Add the beaten egg, water and salt and mix to a dough. Knead until smooth, then set aside to rest for an hour, covered. • Trim, wash and chop the spring onions finely; place half of them in a dish. Chop the well-drained bamboo shoots into small pieces, and add to the spring onions with the chopped pork. Finely chop the chicken breasts and add to the pork with the soy sauce, rice wine, salt and pepper, and combine into a smooth stuffing. • Roll the dough out thinly onto a floured board and cut circles of 8 cm/¾ in diameter and divide the filling among them. • Beat the egg white with 1 tbsp water, and paint the edges of the circles. Fold each circle in two, and press the edges together with a fork. Bring the salted water to the boil, and cook the wontons for 5 minutes, drain in a colander, and set aside. •

Heat the chicken stock; rinse, dry and chop the mustard and cress. Divide the wonton and the remaining spring onions among six soup bowls, pour the chicken stock over, and garnish with mustard and cress.

Lo-Mein Soup

Fast and very easy

Preparation time: 30 minutes
Serves 4

2 litres/4 pt/8 cups water
1 tsp salt
200 g/7 oz Chinese egg noodles
250 g/9 oz pork
3 spring onions
250 g/9 oz Chinese leaves
2 tbsp sesame seed oil
1 litre/2 pt/4 cups hot chicken stock
Pinch each salt and pepper

Bring the salted water to the boil and cook the noodles for about 8 minutes, then drain and set aside. • Cut the pork into ½ cm/¼ in wide strips, and shred the cleaned spring onions and Chinese leaves. • Fry the strips of meat until browned, add the onions and Chinese leaves, and continue cooking for 2 minutes. Add the noodles and pour the chicken stock over. • Season the soup with salt and pepper and serve in warmed soup bowls.

Nabeyaki-Udon Soup

A Japanese speciality

Preparation time: 10 minutes
Serves 4

200 g/7 oz chicken breast fillets
200 g/7 oz button mushrooms
3 spring onions
1 bunch parsley
1 litre/2 pt/4 cups chicken stock
100 g/4 oz spaghetti
4 eggs
2 tbsp soy sauce

Cut the chicken breast fillets into strips 1 cm/½ in wide. Wipe the mushrooms, rinse, slice and set aside. Thoroughly wash the spring onions and cut into rings. Rinse and pat the parsley dry, remove the coarse stems, and chop the leaves finely. • Bring the chicken stock to the boil. Half-cook the spaghetti in the broth (for about 3 minutes) and then add the chicken strips, mushrooms and rings of spring onion. Cook 1 minute more. • Break the eggs one by one into a cup, and slide each one into the soup, rather like poaching eggs, and cook for 3 minutes (the soup should be simmering very gently). Then carefully remove the eggs with a straining spoon and place in soup bowls or plates. • Flavour the soup with the soy sauce and stir in the parsley. Pour the soup over the eggs and serve immediately.

Tip: If you live near a Japanese delicatessen, buy Udon noodles, pale wheat noodles.

Yakko Mein Soup

A Chinese seafood speciality

Preparation time: 40 minutes
Serves 4

6 dried Chinese mushrooms
125 ml/4 fl oz/½ cup warm water
2 litres/4 pt/8 cups water
1 tsp salt
1 tsp oil
200 g/7 oz Chinese noodles
50 g/2 oz lean ham
250 g/9 oz spinach
2.5 cm/1 in piece of fresh root ginger
1 litre/2 pt/4 cups chicken stock
1 dozen fresh oysters
Pinch salt

Cover the dried mushrooms with warm water and leave to soak. • Bring the water to the boil with the salt and oil, and cook the noodles for 8 minutes, drain, set aside and cover to keep warm. • Cut the ham into strips, wash and dry the spinach and tear leaves into small pieces. Peel and finely grate the ginger root. • Drain the mushrooms and cut into shreds. Heat the chicken stock, and add the ham, spinach, mushrooms and shelled oysters. Cook the soup for 2 minutes. • Heat the noodles through in the soup, and stir in the ginger root. Finally, season the soup with salt.

Penne with Mushrooms and Tomatoes

Quick and easy

Preparation time: 1 hour
Serves 4

500 g/18 oz mushrooms
500 g/18 oz tomatoes
1 large onion
1 garlic clove
4 tbsp olive oil
2.5 litres/5 pt/10 cups water
1 tsp salt
225 g/8 oz penne
50 g/2 oz Parmesan cheese
Pinch each herb seasoning and white pepper
½ bunch basil

Wash and dry the mushrooms, and cut into thin slices. Make a slit in the skin of the tomatoes at the bottom, dip briefly into boiling water, remove skins and central stalk. Chop the flesh. • Peel and chop the onion. Peel the garlic, cut into thin slices and fry until transparent in the oil with the chopped onion. • Add the mushrooms and cook, stirring, until the mushroom juice has evaporated completely. • Bring the salted water to the boil and cook the noodles until "al dente," then strain in a colander and set aside, covered, to keep hot. • Stir the tomatoes into the mushroom sauce and cook for 8 minutes. • Grate the Parmesan. Season the sauce with herb seasoning and pepper. Strip the leaves from the sprigs of basil, wash, dry and stir into the sauce. Serve the noodles on warm plates, pouring the sauce over and garnishing each portion with cheese.

Creamy Noodles with Nuts

A Balkan speciality

Preparation time: 15 minutes
Cooking time: 20 minutes
Serves 4

2.5 litres/5 pt/10 cups water
1 tsp salt
225 g/8 oz tagliatelle
200 g/7 oz/2 cups shelled walnuts
2 garlic cloves
50 g/2 oz butter
300 ml/10 fl oz/1¼ cups soured cream

Bring the salted water to the boil and barely cook the noodles: dried tagliatelle needs about 8 minutes, fresh takes only half as long. • Grind 150 g/5 oz/ 1½ cups walnuts in food mill (or processor), peel the garlic and slice thinly. • Fry the ground walnuts and garlic quickly in butter in a large pan. • Drain the noodles and stir into the nuts and garlic mixture, seasoning with salt. • Place the noodles on a warmed dish, sprinkle the rest of the walnuts over them. • Stirring constantly, heat the soured cream very gently—do not allow to boil— and serve separately in a small jug.

Tip: For those who are not cautious about calories, this can be served with cream cheese rather than soured cream. There is also a sweet version of this recipe: instead of salt, flavour with honey or sugar—of course, in this case, omit the garlic!

Spaghetti with Chilli Sauce

Really easy

Preparation time: 1 hour
Serves 4

3 chillies
1 green pepper
2 onions
1 garlic clove
Pinch salt
1 small courgette (zucchini)
2 tomatoes
3 tbsp olive oil
150 g/6 oz/¾ cup canned sweetcorn
2 tbsp tomato purée (paste)
5 tbsp white wine
Pinch black pepper
Pinch dried oregano
2.5 litres/5 pt/10 cups water
1 tsp salt
225 g/8 oz spaghetti

Halve the chillies and green pepper, discard the seeds and white pith, wash, dry and chop very finely. Peel and chop the onions; peel, chop, and crush the garlic with salt. Wash the courgette (zucchini), top and tail, and cut into small cubes. Peel and quarter the tomatoes, discarding the stalky centre; chop the flesh. • Heat 2 tbsp oil in a saucepan and fry the onion until transparent. Add the prepared vegetables and the garlic with the sweetcorn, and cook over a low heat for 5 minutes. • Dilute the tomato purée (paste) with the wine, and stir into the vegetables. Season the sauce with pepper, oregano and salt. • Bring the salted water to the boil, add the remaining oil and the spaghetti, and cook for about 8 minutes, until 'al dente'. • Serve the spaghetti with the sauce.

Chicken Livers and Macaroni

A delicious quick starter

Defrosting time: 30 minutes
Preparation time: 40 minutes
Serves 4

| 300 g/10 oz frozen chicken livers |
| 3 shallots |
| 3 tbsp oil |
| 1 tbsp plain flour |
| 250 ml/8 fl oz/1 cup chicken stock |
| 125 ml/4 fl oz/½ cup red wine |
| 2 tsp paprika |
| 1 tsp red wine vinegar |
| Pinch each salt and freshly ground black pepper |
| 2.5 litres/5 pt/10 cups water |
| 1 tsp salt |
| 225 g/8 oz/1½ cups macaroni |
| 3 tbsp single (light) cream |

Remove the chicken livers from the packets and allow to defrost, covered. • Rinse the livers, pat dry and cut into slices. • Peel the shallots, chop and fry until transparent in the oil. Add the sliced livers to the pan and fry until evenly brown. Stir in the flour and then gradually add the chicken stock and wine. Season the sauce with paprika, vinegar, salt and pepper, and cook for 5 minutes over a very low heat. Then increase the heat to evaporate some of the liquid. • Bring the salted water to the boil, and add the macaroni—do not cook too long, about 10 minutes, or it will be too soft–then drain. Blend the cream into the sauce and serve over the macaroni.

Spaghetti Con Aglio E Olio

A garlic and oil classic

Preparation time: 30 minutes
Serves 4

| 4 garlic cloves |
| 1 bunch parsley |
| 4 tbsp olive oil |
| 1 tiny, hot red chilli |
| 2.5 litres/5 pt/10 cups water |
| 1 tsp salt |
| 1 tbsp vegetable oil |
| 255 g/8 oz spaghetti |
| 4 tbsp grated Parmesan cheese |

Peel and chop the garlic finely. Wash and dry the parsley, and remove the coarse stalks; chop the leaves. • Heat the olive oil in a small pan and fry the garlic gently with the whole chilli, stirring constantly. Take care not to burn the garlic, as it will then taste bitter. Remove the pan from the heat, cover and keep warm. • Bring the salted water to the boil, add the vegetable oil, and cook the spaghetti in the rapidly boiling water for 8 minutes, until tender but not too soft. • Drain the pasta in a colander. Discard the chilli. • Mix the spaghetti with the garlic-oil in a well-warmed serving dish, and garnish with parsley. • Serve with the grated Parmesan cheese.

Penne with Asparagus Tips

Easy and delicious

Preparation time: 45 minutes
Serves 4

400 g/14 oz canned, peeled tomatoes	
1 large garlic clove	
3 anchovy fillets	
1 kg/2¼ lb green asparagus	
3 tbsp olive oil	
2 litres/4 pt/8 cups water	
1½ tsp salt	
1 tsp oil	
225 g/8 oz penne	
Pinch ground black pepper	

Drain the tomatoes in a colander, then chop coarsely. Peel the clove of garlic and cut in half lengthways. Rinse the anchovy fillets under cold water, dry and chop finely. • Thoroughly wash the asparagus under running warm water, and cut the upper green half of each spear into 2.5 cm/1 in pieces. (Use the remaining bottom parts for soup.) • Heat the oil in a large pan and gently cook the garlic, anchovies, tomatoes and asparagus, covered and over a moderate heat, for 15 minutes. • Meanwhile, bring the water to the boil with 1 tsp salt and the oil. Put the pasta into the rapidly boiling water, stir once thoroughly and cook until 'al dente'—approx. 8 minutes. • Drain the pasta and keep warm, covered, in a heated serving dish. • Season the vegetables with salt and pepper and mix with the pasta. Leave the dish covered for 3 minutes for the ingredients to combine well.

Pasta Shells with Courgettes (Zucchini)

Quick and inexpensive

Preparation time: 35 minutes
Serves 4

3 garlic cloves
1 bunch parsley
3 firm courgettes (zucchini)
3 tbsp olive oil
1 tsp fresh oregano or ½ tsp dried
1½ tsp salt
Pinch freshly ground black pepper
1 tsp vegetable oil
2 litres/4 pt/8 cups water
225 g/8 oz pasta shells

Peel the garlic, wash and dry the parsley, chop both finely. Wash, dry and slice the courgettes. • Fry the garlic in olive oil, add the courgettes (zucchini), fry until lightly golden and add the oregano, parsley, ½ tsp salt and the pepper. Keep the vegetables warm. • Add the rest of the salt and the vegetable oil to the water, and bring to the boil. Cook the pasta for about 8 minutes, until tender but not too soft, then drain well in a colander. • Mix the pasta shells with the vegetables and heat through.

Spaghetti with Herbs

A delicious starter

Chilling time: 3 hours
Preparation time: 30 minutes
Serves 4

500 g/18 oz ripe tomatoes
2 garlic cloves
½ large onion
1 stick celery
1 bunch each basil and parsley
3 tbsp olive oil
1 tsp fresh oregano, or ½ tsp dried
½ tsp salt
Pinch freshly ground black pepper
2 litres/4 pt/8 cups water
1 tsp salt
225 g/8 oz spaghetti
1 tsp oil

Score the skins of the tomatoes at the bottom, immerse briefly in boiling water, peel, chop the flesh, discarding the seeds and stalky centre part. Allow to drain in a colander. Peel and crush the garlic and place in a large serving dish. Peel and finely chop the onion. Wash and dry the celery, remove the coarse stringy parts, and slice thinly. Wash the basil and parsley, pat dry, chop finely and mix with the tomato pieces, onion, celery, olive oil, and the fresh or dried oregano. Season the vegetable mixture with salt and pepper and chill in refrigerator for 3 hours. • Cook the spaghetti in boiling salted water with the oil for about 8 minutes, or until the pasta is 'al dente', then drain well and serve immediately with the tomato and herb mixture.

Homemade Tagliatelle with Spinach

Delicious and nutritious

Preparation time: 1½ hours
Serves 4

200 g/7 oz/1¾ cups plain flour
2 eggs
½ tsp salt
750 g/1 lb 12 oz young spinach
2 garlic cloves
1 tbsp oil
40 g/1½ oz butter
1 tsp salt
Pinch freshly grated nutmeg
Pinch freshly ground black pepper
3 litres/6 pt/12 cups water
1 tsp salt
50 g/2 oz/½ cup grated Parmesan cheese

Make a firm, pliable dough with the flour, eggs and salt; shape dough into a roll and leave to rest under an inverted dish for 1 hour. • Clean the spinach and steam gently in its own juice until tender, then chop finely. • Peel and halve the garlic cloves. Heat the oil and half the butter in a saucepan, fry the garlic until golden, and discard. Place the spinach in the oil with the salt, nutmeg and pepper and cook, covered, for 5 minutes over a very low heat. • Roll out the dough thinly on a floured work surface, roll up, and cut into strips. Spread the strips over the work surface to dry briefly. • Bring the salted water to the boil. Cook the tagliatelle in the rapidly boiling water for 5 minutes, or until 'al dente', drain in a colander and mix with the remaining butter in a heated serving dish. • Spread the spinach over the pasta and sprinkle with grated Parmesan cheese.

Tagliatelle with Tomatoes, Mushrooms and Sage

An Italian speciality

Preparation time: 1 hour
Serves 4

| 1 large onion |
| 2 garlic cloves |
| 400 g/14 oz button mushrooms |
| 1 tbsp lemon juice |
| 2 tomatoes |
| 40 g/1½ oz butter |
| Pinch each salt, sugar and black pepper |
| 2 litres/4 pt/8 cups water |
| 1 tsp salt |
| 1 tsp oil |
| 225 g/8 oz tagliatelle |
| ½ bunch sage |

Peel and chop the onion. Peel and chop the garlic very finely. Clean the mushrooms, slice vertically and sprinkle with lemon juice. Score around the tomato skins, dip into boiling water, skin, quarter, discard the centre stalky part, and chop the flesh. • Heat the butter, and fry the chopped onion until transparent. • Add the mushrooms and the garlic, and cook over a low heat for 10 minutes. • Add the tomatoes and season the vegetables with salt, sugar and pepper. • Bring the salted water to the boil, and add the oil. Cook the tagliatelle for 8 minutes until tender. • Rip the sage leaves from the stalk, wash, dry, and shred. • Rinse the pasta in a colander, and leave to drain, before mixing with the vegetables. Sprinkle the sage on top. • Serve the pasta immediately in a warmed dish.

Pasta Nests with Mussels

Simple and quick

Preparation time: 40 minutes
Serves 4

| 2.5 litres/5 pt/10 cups water |
| 1½ tsp salt |
| 4 nests of tagliatelle, each about 65 g/2½ oz |
| 200 g/7 oz frozen mussels, thawed |
| 5 anchovy fillets |
| 2 tbsp capers |
| 150 ml /5 fl oz/⅔ cup single (light) cream |
| ½ tsp English mustard |
| Pinch each salt and black pepper |
| A few drops lemon juice |

Bring the salted water to the boil, and place the pasta nests in the saucepan, turning down the heat a little, so that the pasta cooks in about 8 minutes. Then drain the tagliatelle in a colander, reserving the water. Keep the pasta covered and hot. • Chop the anchovy fillets very finely and mix with the drained capers and the mussels. • Heat the cream very gently in a saucepan and add the mustard, seasoning, lemon juice and mussel and anchovy mixture. • Serve the pasta nests individually with the mussel sauce.

Pasta with Broccoli and Garlic

Very simple

Preparation time: 1 hour
Serves 4

3 garlic cloves
3 anchovy fillets
1 kg/2¼ lb broccoli
2 litres/4 pt/8 cups water
1 tsp salt
225 g/8 oz macaroni
3 tbsp olive oil
1 pinch cayenne pepper

Peel the garlic and chop finely. Rinse the anchovy fillets, dry and chop. Wash the broccoli thoroughly and drain well. Trim the stalks and cut the broccoli into 5 cm/2 in pieces (chop thicker pieces shorter, so that the cooking time is the same). • Bring the salted water to the boil, and cook the broccoli, covered, over a moderate heat for about 10 minutes, then drain in a colander, reserving the cooking liquid. Keep warm. • Cook the pasta pipes in the reserved broccoli cooking water for approx. 8 minutes, until 'al dente'. • Meanwhile, heat the olive oil in a small saucepan. Let the garlic, anchovies and cayenne pepper fry gently over low heat for 15 minutes, stirring. • Drain the pasta in a colander, place in a preheated serving dish, mix with broccoli and the anchovy sauce and allow to stand for 5 minutes, for the flavours to mingle. Mix once more before serving.

Tomatoes and Gnocchi

A superb accompaniment

Preparation time: 50 minutes
Serves 4

300 g/11 oz/2¾ cups flour
½ tsp salt
1 pinch saffron
800 g/1¾ lb tomatoes
3 garlic cloves
3 tbsp olive oil
1½ tbsp chopped basil
½ tsp salt
Pinch white pepper
1 tsp chopped fresh oregano
3 litres/6 pt/12 cups water
1½ tsp salt
2 tbsp grated Feta

Sift the flour into a bowl and add the salt. Soak the saffron in a little water and add to the flour. Gradually add enough water to form a dough. Knead the dough well, shape into ropes 1 cm/½ in thick, and cut the ropes into pieces 5 cm/2 in long. Score around the bottom of the tomatoes, and dip into boiling water, skin, chop up, discarding the hard core. Peel and quarter the garlic. • Heat the oil in a large saucepan, fry the garlic, stirring, and then discard. Add the basil, the tomatoes and the salt and pepper. Stir well and cook gently for 30 minutes. Last, mix in the oregano. • To cook the gnocchi, bring the salted water to the boil. Cook the gnocchi until they rise to the surface. Drain, mix carefully with the tomato mixture and serve, sprinkled with Feta cheese.

Potato Gnocchi

A good and unusual accompaniment

Preparation time: 1¼ hours
Serves 4–6

1 kg/2¼ lb floury potatoes
1 tsp salt
150 g/5 oz Parmesan cheese
250–300 g/9–11 oz/2¼–2¾ cups flour
4 litres/8 pt water
2 tsp salt
150 g/5 oz butter

Peel the potatoes, wash and cut into even, large pieces; cook in salted water, covered, for 20 minutes. • Grate the Parmesan cheese. Mash and then coarsely sieve the potatoes and place on a floured board. Leave to cool. Season with a little salt, and knead into the potatoes as much flour as it takes to produce a smooth, but not too firm, dough. Leave the potato dough to rest for 10 minutes, then divide into 8 portions, and shape these into rolls as thick as a thumb. Cut them into 2½ cm/1 in lengths, and press lightly with a fork, to make a faint pattern. • Bring the salted water to the boil in a large saucepan. Carefully slide the gnocchi in, and stir gently with a fork. When the gnocchi rise to the surface, they are cooked. Remove with a straining spoon and drain. Butter a well warmed serving dish thickly, and layer the gnocchi with grated Parmesan cheese and the rest of the butter. • Serve hot.

Cornmeal Gnocchi

An unusual accompaniment

Preparation time: 1 hour
Serves 4

1.25 litres/2½ pt/5 cups water
1 tbsp salt
350 g/12 oz/2½ cups coarse-ground cornmeal
100 g/4 oz Parmesan cheese
100 g/4 oz melted butter
250 ml/8 fl oz/1 cup single (light) cream
Butter to grease baking dish

Bring the salted water to the boil in a deep pan. Gradually add the cornmeal and beat with an egg whisk to separate the grains, and prevent lumps. Cook over low heat for 45 minutes, by which time it should have a thick porridge consistency. • Meanwhile grate the Parmesan and butter a shallow gratin dish generously. Preheat the oven to 200°C/400°F/Gas Mark 6. • Using a tablespoon repeatedly dipped in hot water, shape gnocchi from the cornmeal, and gently slide into the gratin dish. Cover the first layer of gnocchi with Parmesan, and the second with melted butter. Pour the cream over the final layer. • Bake the cornmeal gnocchi in the oven for 5 minutes.

Fettucine with Garlic Butter

Quick and inexpensive

Preparation time: 35 minutes
Serves 4

2.5 litres/5 pt/10 cups water
1½ tsp salt
250 g/9 oz tagliatelle
50 g/2 oz butter
2 tbsp pine kernels
50 g/2 oz grated Parmesan cheese
2 garlic cloves
Pinch of mixed herbs

Bring the water to the boil and add the salt. Cook the pasta for approx. 8 minutes until 'al dente'. • Melt 1 teaspoon butter in a small saucepan, and brown the pine kernels lightly. • Grate the cheese and peel and crush the garlic. Blend the garlic with the remaining butter and herbs. • Mix the well-drained pasta well with the garlic butter, and place in a heated serving dish. • Sprinkle the toasted pine kernels over the pasta. Garnish the pasta with the grated Parmesan and serve immediately.

Tip: Instead of pine kernels, chopped walnuts are also very tasty.

Fettucine with Peppers

Quick and inexpensive

Preparation time: 35 minutes
Cooking time: 20 minutes
Serves 4

500 g/18 oz yellow peppers
300 g/11 oz tomatoes
2 large onions
1 chilli
50 g/2 oz lean streaky bacon
3 tbsp sunflower oil
2.5 litres/5 pt/10 cups water
1½ tsp salt
250 g/9 oz tagliatelle
50 g/2 oz/½ cup grated Parmesan cheese

Wash the yellow peppers, halve, remove centre core, white pithy parts and seeds. Cut into narrow strips. Score the skin at the bottom of the tomatoes and dip them briefly in boiling water, remove skins and stalky part in middle, and chop the flesh. Peel and finely chop the onions. Wash the chilli and slice into narrow rings. Chop the bacon. • Heat the oil in a pan, and fry the bacon until crispy. Add the onions and fry until transparent, stirring, and then add the peppers, tomatoes, and chilli. Leave the vegetables to steam in their own juice gently for 15 minutes. • Bring the water to the boil, add the salt and the tagliatelle, and cook until 'al dente', then strain and set aside. • Season the sauce. Turn the pasta into a warmed dish. Top with the sauce and Parmesan cheese before serving.

Tip: Fettucine is simply another word for tagliatelle; the term is commonly used in Rome and other central parts of Italy.

Hah Gavs

A Chinese speciality

Preparation time: 1¾ hours
Serves 4-6

250 ml/8 fl oz/1 cup water
150 g/5 oz/1¼ cups plain flour
5 canned water chestnuts
½ bunch parsley
25 g/1 oz lean ham
150 g/6 oz/1 cup peeled prawns
Pinch salt
½ tsp sugar
4 tbsp sesame seed oil
8 tbsp soy sauce

Bring the water to the boil. Sift the flour into a bowl, and stir in the boiling water, and make a pliable dough. Shape into a roll 2.5 cm/1 in thick and leave to rest covered by a tea towel for an hour. • Drain the water chestnuts

and cut into very small pieces. Wash and pat dry the parsley, remove the coarse stem and chop the leaves finely. Chop the ham and prawns. Mix all the chopped ingredients together and season with salt and sugar. • Cut pieces of dough the size of a walnut from the roll, shape into balls in the palm of the hand and flatten. Place the stuffing in the centre, make each circle into a little "pouch" and press the edges together. • In a large pan bring 5 cm/2 in water to the boil. Place dumplings on a piece of oiled greaseproof paper and then steam over the boiling water in bamboo or metal steamers for 10 minutes. • Mix the soy sauce with the remaining sesame seed oil and offer as an accompaniment to the dumplings.

Jao Mais

A Chinese speciality

Preparation time: 1¾ hours
Serves 4-6

3 dried Chinese mushrooms
300 g/11 oz/2¾ cups plain flour
1 egg
125 ml/4 fl oz/½ cup water
½ tsp salt
200 g/7 oz prawns
200 g/7 oz chopped pork
½ tsp each salt and pepper
Pinch white pepper
4 tbsp each sake (rice wine), sesame seed oil and soy sauce

Leave the mushrooms to soak in lukewarm water. • Sift the flour into a bowl. Beat the egg with the water and salt, add to the flour and make a pliable dough. Leave to rest covered by a tea towel for an hour. • Chop the prawns and the drained mushrooms finely, and mix with the chopped pork, salt, pepper and sake. • Shape the dough into a roll approx. 2.5 cm/1 in thick, and divide into 40 small balls. Roll the balls out very thinly and dust with flour. • Divide the filling among the circles of dough. Wet the edges and fold the circles into crescent shapes, pressing the edges together. Place the "pouches" on pieces of oiled greaseproof paper and steam in bamboo steamers for 15 minutes. • Mix the soy sauce with the remaining sesame seed oil and offer as an accompaniment to the dumplings.

Crispy Won Tons

A famous Chinese speciality

Preparation time: 2½ hours
Serves 4–6

---

300 g/11 oz/2¾ cups flour

1 egg

125 ml/4 fl oz/½ cup water

½ tsp salt

1 spring onion

100 g/4 oz canned bamboo shoots

275 g/10 oz minced pork

1 tbsp soy sauce

1 tbsp sake (rice wine) or dry sherry

Pinch each salt and freshly ground black pepper

1 egg white

225 g/8 oz canned stoned plums, with juice reserved

Pinch each cinnamon and grated lemon peel

Corn oil for deep frying

Sift the flour into a bowl. Beat the egg with the water and salt, add to the flour and make a pliable dough; knead until elastic and smooth–this takes 10 to 15 minutes. Leave to rest covered by an inverted dish or tea towel for an hour. • Wash the spring onion thoroughly, dry and cut into thin rings. Cut the bamboo shoots into tiny pieces. Mix the pork with the soy sauce, the sake or sherry, the salt and pepper; then combine with the spring onion and bamboo shoots. • Shape the pasta dough into 2.5 cm/1 in thick roll and slice into approx. 40 pieces.

Shape into balls and then roll each out on a floured board very thinly, and dust with flour. Beat the egg white and 1 tbsp water together and paint the edges of the circles. Divide the filling between the circles and fold them together into crescent shapes, pressing the edges together firmly with a fork. Leave to rest until the plum sauce is ready. • Purée the plums with the cinnamon and grated lemon rind in the blender, and pass through a sieve. Sweeten the sauce to taste and thin with a little juice if necessary. • Heat the oil in a deep-fat fryer to 180°C/350°F and fry the won tons until golden. Turn during cooking. • Serve the won tons either hot or cold with the plum sauce.

Tip: To avoid drying out the dough slices too quickly after rolling, fill and seal them in batches, covering the remaining pasta circles with a damp tea towel. If the pasta is too dry, it will not fold over the filling as well as it should. If desired, chopped bean sprouts can be used instead of bamboo shoots.

Kuo Tiehs

An Asian speciality

Preparation time: 2 hours
Serves 4-6

300 g/11 oz/2¾ cups plain flour	
250 ml/8 fl oz/1 cup water	
250 g/9 oz Chinese leaves	
2 spring onions	
250 g/9 oz minced pork	
2 tbsp soy sauce	
1 tbsp rice wine	
½ tsp each salt and sugar	
6 tbsp oil	

Divide the flour into two separate bowls. Bring 125 ml/4 fl oz/½ cup water to the boil, stir 125 ml/4 fl oz/½ cup cold water into half the flour, and mix the boiling water with the other half of flour. Knead both doughs together and leave to rest, covered, while preparing the filling. • Wash the Chinese leaves, shred, and cook with 4 tbsp water in a covered saucepan over a low heat for 10 minutes. • Clean the spring onions and cut into thin rings; mix with the minced pork, the soy sauce, rice wine, salt, sugar and the Chinese leaves. • Shape the dough into a 2.5 cm/ 1 in thick roll, cut walnut-sized pieces off, and roll out thinly on a floured surface. • Divide the filling among the circles of dough. Gather the dough circles around the filling like small drawstring bags, and leave to rest covered with a tea towel on a floured board for 20 minutes. • Heat half the oil in a pan, and place the pasta "bags" in the pan. Add enough cold water to come half-way up the bags, and steam for 3 minutes in the covered pan. Then drain off the liquid. Trickle the remaining oil over the bags and cook until crisp for 10–12 minutes. • Serve with Chinese mustard or soy sauce.

Pasta with Sauces and Ragoûts

Spaghetti with Gorgonzola Sauce

Simple and popular

Preparation time: 30 minutes
Serves 4

1 small onion
1–2 garlic cloves
3 tbsp olive oil
1 tsp plain flour
500 ml/16 fl oz/2 cups single (light) cream
125 ml/4 fl oz/½ cup dry white wine
300 g/11 oz Gorgonzola cheese
50 g/2 oz/½ cup pine kernels
400 g/14 oz spaghetti
4 litres/8 pt water
2 tsp salt
½ tsp mixed dried herbs

Peel and chop the onion and garlic very finely and fry quickly in oil. Shake the flour over, and make a sauce with the cream and white wine. • Stir 200 g/7 oz Gorgonzola and the pine kernels into the sauce, and heat for 10 minutes. • Cook spaghetti in boiling salted water until 'al dente', drain, and mix with sauce and herbs. Sprinkle remaining cheese on top.

Spaghetti with Basil

Very easy and quick

Preparation time: 30 minutes
Serves 4

2 shallots
1–2 garlic cloves
2 tbsp olive oil
250 ml/8 fl oz/1 cup single (light) cream
150 ml/5 fl oz/⅔ cup soured cream
2 bunches basil
Pinch each salt and freshly ground white pepper

1–2 tsp lemon juice
1 egg yolk
400 g/14 oz spaghetti, cooked

Fry finely chopped shallots and garlic in oil and add creams. Stir in basil, seasonings, lemon juice and egg yolk. Combine sauce with cooked pasta.

Spaghetti with Salmon Sauce

A delicious, rich dish

Preparation time: 45 minutes
Serves 4

125 ml/4 fl oz/½ cup dry white wine
½ tsp each salt and peppercorns
½ bunch tarragon
350 g/12 oz fresh salmon
500 ml/16 fl oz/2 cups single (light) cream
150 g/5 oz carrots

400 g/14 oz spaghetti
4 litres/8 pt water
2 tsp salt
1 tbsp oil
Pinch white pepper
25 g/1 oz cold butter

Bring the wine to the boil with the salt, peppercorns and 1 sprig tarragon, and poach the salmon in this for 3–5 minutes, before flaking. • Strain the stock through a sieve and boil down to half the quantity. • Add the cream and reduce again to half the quantity. • Scrape the carrots and slice thinly; blanch for 2 minutes. • Cook the spaghetti in the salted water and oil until 'al dente'; drain. • Finely chop remaining tarragon, and mix into the cream sauce, season with salt and pepper. Add butter a teaspoon at a time. Briefly heat salmon and carrots in the sauce before serving with the spaghetti.

Wholewheat Spaghetti with Tofu Sauce

Complete meal, easy

Preparation time: 1 hour
Serves 4

300 g/11 oz tofu (soy curd)
2 tbsp soy sauce
3 tbsp sesame seeds
Pinch freshly ground black pepper
3 tomatoes
1 onion
500 g/18 oz cucumber
50 g/2 oz butter
4 litres/8 pt water
2 tsp salt
400 g/14 oz wholewheat spaghetti
100 g/4 oz crumbled Feta
250 ml/8 fl oz/1 cup soured cream
4 tbsp fresh dill, finely chopped
1 tsp paprika

Drain the tofu, cut into small cubes, and mix in a small bowl with the soy sauce, the sesame seeds and the pepper. • Slit around the tomato skins and dip in boiling water; peel and remove the stalky centre. Dice the flesh. Peel the cucumber and dice. • Peel the onion, finely dice and fry until transparent in the butter. Add the tofu mixture and fry 2–3 minutes, turning. Add the cucumber and tomatoes to the tofu and cook together over a low heat for 10–15 minutes. • Bring the water to the boil, add salt and spaghetti. Cook until 'al dente' then drain in a colander, rinse briefly with cold water and keep hot in a warmed serving dish. • Remove the tofu mixture from the heat, stir in the cheese, soured cream and dill. Season with the paprika and a little more soy sauce. • Serve the sauce on top of the spaghetti.

Pasta Casserole with Mushrooms

Easy supper dish

Preparation time: 40 minutes
Serves 4

600 g/1 lb 5 oz mushrooms
40 g/1½ oz butter
Pinch each salt and black pepper
2 tsp paprika
3 tbsp tomato purée (paste)
250 ml/8 fl oz/1 cup soured cream
4 litres/8 pt water
2 tsp salt
400 g/14 oz macaroni
½ bunch parsley
Grated Parmesan, to serve

Rinse the mushrooms in cold water, pat dry and chop. • Heat the butter in a pan, fry the mushrooms with the salt, pepper and paprika. Stir the tomato purée (paste) into the cream and mix both into the mushrooms. Leave the mushrooms to simmer over a low heat while pasta cooks. • Bring the salted water to the boil and drop in the pasta to cook for 8 minutes. • Drain the cooked pasta in a colander and mix with the mushroom sauce in a heated serving dish, sprinkled with chopped parsley. • Serve with grated Parmesan cheese.

Pasta with Ham Sauce

Inexpensive and easy to make

Preparation time: 30 minutes
Serves 4

100 g/4 oz lean ham
4 shallots
1 garlic clove
40 g/1½ oz butter
125 ml/4 fl oz/½ cup hot beef stock
250 ml/8 fl oz/1 cup soured cream
4 litres/8 pt water
2 tsp salt
400 g/14 oz pasta spirals
1 egg yolk
1 bunch chives

Cut the ham into very fine strips; peel and finely chop the shallots and garlic. • Melt the butter, and fry the shallots and garlic until transparent, then add the ham. Pour in the beef stock and let it all cook together. Stir in the soured cream and leave the liquid to reduce, uncovered, while cooking the pasta. • Bring the salted water to the boil, and cook the pasta until 'al dente'. • Beat the egg yolk with 2 tbsp hot sauce, and then blend into the cream sauce. Do not allow to return to the boil. • Wash, dry and chop the chives. • Drain the pasta in a colander, mix into the cream sauce and serve in a heated dish, sprinkled with chives. • A tasty dressed tomato salad with mozzarella cheese, onion rings and fresh basil goes very well with this.

Spaghetti with Anchovies

An Italian speciality

Preparation time: 1 hour
Serves 4

5 anchovy fillets
300 g/11 oz ripe tomatoes
½ bunch parsley
50 g/2 oz/½ cup black olives, stoned
2–3 garlic cloves
1 tbsp capers
2 tbsp olive oil
Pinch salt
½ tsp fresh or pinch dried oregano
Pinch chilli powder or cayenne pepper
400 g/14 oz spaghetti
4 litres/8 pt water
1 tsp salt

Rinse the anchovy fillets, dry and finely chop. Slit the tomatoes around the bottom, and briefly dip into boiling water. Remove skins and the stalky centre. Chop the tomato flesh. Wash and dry the parsley, and chop, along with the pitted olives, peeled garlic and the drained capers. • Heat the oil and stir-fry the anchovies, parsley, olives, garlic and capers together for about 5 minutes, and then add the tomatoes. Season with salt, oregano and chilli or cayenne. Leave the sauce to thicken over a medium heat for 30 minutes. • Cook the spaghetti in boiling water for about 8 minutes, until just firm to the bite. • Stir the drained spaghetti into the sauce.

Wholemeal Pasta with Veal Stew

A good winter dish

Marinating time: 1 hour
Preparation time: 1¼ hour
Serves 4

| 500 g/1 lb 2 oz veal |
| 2 tbsp soy sauce |
| 2 pinches white pepper |
| 1 onion |
| 1 bay leaf |
| 2 cloves |
| 500 g/18 oz each courgettes (zucchini) and tomatoes |
| 1 tbsp melted butter |
| 300 g/11 oz green pasta |
| 3 litres/6 pt water |
| 1½ tsp salt |
| 1 tbsp plain flour |
| 120 ml/4 fl oz/½ cup soured cream |
| ½ tsp each chopped fresh rosemary, marjoram and basil |
| 2 tsp freshly chopped lemon balm mint or parsley |

Cut the meat into 2 cm/¾ in cubes, mix with soy sauce and 1 pinch pepper and leave to marinate for 1 hour. • Slowly cook the whole onion, bay leaf and cloves in the butter. Clean the courgettes (zucchini), top and tail and chop coarsely. Skin the tomatoes and quarter, discarding the stalky centres. • Fry the meat in the butter for 5 minutes, then add the courgettes (zucchini), tomatoes and a little more pepper, and cook for 1 hour. • Cook the pasta in boiling salted water for about 10 minutes. • Stir the flour into the soured cream, blend into the stew and leave to cook for 2 more minutes. Discard the onion and mix in the herbs. • Drain the pasta in a colander and serve with the stew on top.

Babuschka-Pasta with Chinese Leaves

A complete meal in itself

Preparation time: 1 hour
Serves 4

| 150 g/5 oz/1¼ cups wholemeal flour |
| 100 g/4 oz/1 cup buckwheat flour |
| ½ tsp sea salt |
| 3 tbsp sunflower oil |
| 250 ml/8 fl oz/1 cup lukewarm water |
| 50 g/2 oz/⅓ cup sunflower seeds |
| 3 cooking apples |
| 500 g/18 oz Chinese leaves |
| 2.5 litres/5 pt/10 cups water |
| 1 tsp salt |
| 40 g/1½ oz butter |
| 125 ml/4 fl oz/½ cup soured cream |
| 1 tsp each herbs and paprika |
| 1 tsp honey |
| 2 tbs freshly chopped parsley |

To make the pasta, mix all the flour with the salt, oil and water to a smooth but firm dough. Invert a warmed dish over it. • Toast the sunflower seeds in a pan. Wash, peel, quarter, core and dice the apples and place in a saucepan with 250 ml/8 fl oz/1 cup water. Clean and finely shred the Chinese leaves, add to the apples and cook for 15–20 minutes. • Roll out the pasta dough in 4 portions the thickness of a knife, and cut into strips 1 cm/⅓ in wide. Leave the pasta to dry for 5 minutes, then cook in swiftly boiling salted water; it is cooked when it rises to the surface. Drain the pasta and mix with the butter and sunflower seeds. • Blend together the cream, herbs, paprika, honey and parsley and stir into the apple and Chinese leaves mixture. Serve with the pasta.

Noodles with Sovrito Sauce

Quick and economical

Preparation time: 45 minutes
Serves 4

1 thin rasher of streaky bacon
50 g/2 oz back bacon
3 shallots
1 small green pepper
2 large tomatoes
1 garlic clove
125 ml/4 fl oz/½ cup beef stock
400 g/14 oz wide noodles
4 litres/8 pt water
2 tsp salt
8 black olives
Pinch each cayenne pepper and dried thyme

Shred all the bacon and fry. •
Peel the shallots, finely chop and sauté in the bacon fat until transparent. Halve the pepper, discard the central core, the pith, seeds, etc., and dice. Slit the tomatoes, dip into boiling water briefly, remove the skins and stalky centre and dice the flesh. Peel and finely chop the garlic, and add with the diced green pepper and the tomato to the bacon and onion mixture. Pour the beef stock over and cook the vegetables for 10–15 minutes. •
Cook the pasta for 8 minutes in salted water until 'al dente'. •
Halve and stone the olives, mix into the vegetable sauce and season with salt, cayenne and thyme.
• Serve the sauce on top of the noodles on a warmed serving plate.

Spaghetti Bolognaise

An all-time favourite

Preparation time: 10 minutes
Cooking time: 40 minutes
Serves 4

100 g/4 oz bacon
2 onions
1 carrot
3 sticks celery
1 bunch parsley
3 tbsp olive oil
300 g/10 oz minced beef
100 g/4 oz minced pork
2 tbsp tomato purée (paste)
300 ml/10 fl oz/1¼ cups hot beef stock
500 ml/16 fl oz/2 cups dry white wine
1 bay leaf
½ tsp salt
Pinch black pepper
Pinch sugar
4 litres/8 pt water
2 tsp salt
400 g/14 oz spaghetti
100 g/4 oz chicken livers
2 tsp butter

Cut the bacon into narrow strips, peel and finely chop the onions, scrape, wash and dice the carrot. Wash the celery and finely slice. Wash, pat dry and chop the parsley. • Heat 2 tbsp oil in a large saucepan. Brown the minced meat, stirring, add the bacon and onions and brown for 3 more minutes. • Add the carrot, celery, parsley, tomato purée (paste), stock, wine, bay leaf, salt, pepper and sugar. Cook the sauce gently for 30 minutes over a low heat. • Bring the water to the boil, and add the salt, the remaining oil and the spaghetti and cook until 'al dente', about 8 minutes. • Fry the chicken livers in 1 tsp butter, finely chop and add to the sauce. • Drain the spaghetti in a colander, add the rest of the butter and serve with the sauce on top.

Pasta with Basil Sauce (Pesto)

An Italian classic recipe

Preparation time: 30 minutes
Serves 4

2 bunches basil
2–3 garlic cloves
1 tbsp pine kernels
Pinch salt
100 g/4 oz/1 cup freshly grated Parmesan cheese
250 ml/8 fl oz/1 cup olive oil
4 litres/8 pt water
2 tsp salt
400 g/14 oz pasta (spaghetti, macaroni or tagliatelle)
1 tbsp butter

Wash the basil and strip the leaves from the stems. Peel and coarsely chop the garlic, and crush to a paste with the basil, pine kernels and salt. Add the Parmesan. Add the oil, at first drop by drop, but then in a steady stream, stirring it into the paste. • Bring the water to the boil and add pasta and salt, cook until 'al dente', drain and rinse with warm water. Mix in the butter, and serve the pasta accompanied by the pesto.

Pasta with Salsa Di Pomodori

An Italian speciality

Preparation time: 50 minutes
Serves 4

1 kg/2¼ lb very ripe tomatoes
2 onions
2 tbsp olive oil
1 bunch basil
2 tbsp tomato purée (paste)
1 tsp sugar
½ tsp salt
Pinch freshly ground black pepper
4 litres/8 pt water
2 tsp salt
400 g/14 oz pasta (spaghetti, macaroni or tagliatelle)
1 tsp butter
100 g/4 oz/1 cup freshly grated Parmesan cheese

Wash the tomatoes, discard the stalks, and chop into small pieces. Peel and finely chop the onions and fry in the oil until transparent. Add the tomatoes and cook, covered, for 10 minutes. • Wash the basil and strip the leaves from the stems. Set aside some leaves to garnish the dish, but chop the rest and add to the onions and tomatoes with the tomato purée (paste), sugar, salt and pepper. Leave the sauce to cook for 30 minutes, stirring occasionally. Strain and return to the pan. • Bring the water to the boil, cook the pasta until 'al dente', then drain and mix with butter. Serve the tomato sauce on the pasta with grated cheese.

Pasta with Tuna Sauce

Quick and economical

Preparation time: 30 minutes
Serves 4

| 2 garlic cloves |
| 300 g/10 oz canned tuna |
| 400 g/14 oz tomatoes |
| 1 tbsp olive oil |
| Salt |
| 3 litres/6 pt/12 cups water |
| 1 tbsp oil |
| 300 g/10 oz tagliatelle |
| 1 bunch parsley |
| A few basil leaves |

Peel and finely chop the garlic. Drain and flake the tuna. • Slit around the tomato skins at the rounded end, submerge in boiling water, allow to cool and remove the skins, and cut away the hard stalky centre. • Heat the olive oil and fry the garlic until golden. Add the pieces of tomato, the tuna and salt and cook covered for 20 minutes over a very low heat. • Bring the water to the boil with a little salt and oil. Add the noodles, stir thoroughly once, and cook until 'al dente'. • Wash the parsley, dry, discard the coarse stems and chop the leaves, and stir into the tuna sauce. • Drain the pasta, then place in a pre-heated dish and cover with the tuna sauce; garnish with the basil leaves.

Tagliatelle Alla Emilia-Romagna

A very simple Italian speciality

Preparation time: 40 minutes
Serves 4

| 50 g/2 oz streaky bacon |
| 3 litres/6 pt/12 cups water |
| 5 tsp oil |
| 300 g/10 oz tagliatelle |
| 4 tbsp single (light) cream |
| 300 g/10 oz/2 cups frozen peas |

Dice the bacon finely, removing bone and rind. • Bring the water to the boil, add 2 tsp of oil, salt and pasta, stir thoroughly once and cook until 'al dente'. • Heat the remaining oil in a pan and brown the bacon until crispy. Add the cream and frozen peas, stir and cook over a low heat for 5 minutes. • Drain the pasta in a colander, and mix with the sauce in a warm serving dish.

Spaghetti Alla Carbonara

Another all-time favourite

Preparation time: 30 minutes
Serves 4

3 litres/6 pt/12 cups water
1½ tsp salt
1 tbsp vegetable oil
400 g/14 oz spaghetti
50 g/2 oz lean bacon
2 garlic cloves
1 tbsp olive oil
2 eggs, beaten
4 tbsp single cream
50 g/2 oz/½ cup grated Parmesan cheese
½ tsp salt
Pinch white pepper

Bring the water to the boil, and add salt, vegetable oil and spaghetti. Cook for 8 minutes until 'al dente'. • Dice the bacon, peel and quarter the garlic. • Heat the olive oil in a large pan, and brown the garlic, stirring frequently; then discard the garlic. Fry the bacon until crispy and brown. • Mix the eggs with cream, cheese, salt and pepper in a preheated dish. Drain the spaghetti, add to the bacon in the pan, heat once more, stirring, and then turn into a serving dish and stir in the cream and cheese mixture. Serve immediately.

Spaghetti Alla Napoletana

Economical Neapolitan speciality

Preparation time: 40 minutes
Serves 4

1 onion
1 tbsp olive oil
1 sprig each parsley and basil
400 g/14 oz tomatoes
Pinch paprika
Salt and sugar
3 litres/6 pt/12 cups water
1 tsp vegetable oil
400 g/14 oz spaghetti
50 g/2 oz Parmesan cheese

Peel and finely chop the onion and fry in the olive oil until golden. • Wash the herbs, dry, remove coarse stems and chop. Add to the onion. • Slit the tomato skins, immerse in boiling water, peel and chop, removing the stalk and hard centre. Add tomatoes to the onions, with the paprika and a pinch of salt and sugar. Cover and cook over a low heat for 10 minutes. • Cook the spaghetti for 8 minutes until 'al dente' in boiling water with salt and oil. Grate the Parmesan. Serve the drained spaghetti in a preheated serving dish mixed with the tomato sauce. • Serve the Parmesan cheese separately.

Stufatu

A very tasty recipe

Preparation time: 2½ hours
Serves 6

300 g/10 oz lean stewing beef
300 g/10 oz lean loin of pork
50 g/2 oz streaky bacon
4 large tomatoes
1 large onion
4 garlic cloves
4 tbsp olive oil
125 ml/4 fl oz/½ cup dry white wine
1 tsp salt
2 pinches white pepper
3 litres/6 pt/12 cups water
1½ tsp salt
500 g/18 oz macaroni
50 g/2 oz/½ cup grated Gruyère cheese
2 tbsp chopped parsley

Cube the meat, removing fat and sinews, cut the bacon into strips. Peel the tomatoes and cut into small pieces. • Peel the onion and garlic and fry in oil until transparent. Add the cubes of meat and brown, stirring. Add the tomatoes and bacon, and cook briefly together, before adding the wine. Season with salt and pepper. Add enough water just to cover the meat. Braise gently for 2 hours over a low heat. • Bring the salted water to the boil and cook the macaroni for about 10 minutes until 'al dente'. • Heat the oven to 200°C/400°F/Gas Mark 6. Drain the macaroni. Place the meat in a large ovenproof dish, top with the macaroni and then the cheese. Bake until the cheese is golden. • Serve garnished with parsley.

Tagliatelle with Pork

An African speciality

Preparation time: 1 hour
Serves 4

500 g/18 oz pork fillet
1 large onion
2 tbsp corn oil
3 large beef tomatoes
2 garlic cloves
1 red chilli
Salt and pepper
2 tsp lemon juice
2 tsp honey
1 tbsp Worcestershire sauce
250 ml/8 fl oz/1 cup hot vegetable stock
3 litres/6 pt/12 cups water
1½ tsp salt
300 g/10 oz tagliatelle
100 g/4 oz/1 cup grated cheddar cheese

Wash the meat, dry and cut into 2 cm/¾ in cubes. Peel and chop the onion and fry in the oil with the meat. Peel the tomatoes, cut into pieces, discarding the central stalky part, and add tomatoes to the meat. Peel and crush the garlic. Halve and wash the chilli, finely chop and add to the meat. • Stir in the salt, pepper, lemon juice, Worcestershire sauce, vegetable stock and stew gently for 30 minutes. • Bring the salted water to the boil, add the pasta and cook for about 8 minutes, until 'al dente'. Drain in a colander and serve topped with the meat sauce. • Sprinkle cheese over just before serving.

Wholemeal Spaghetti with Tofu Bolognaise

A meal in itself

Preparation time: 35 minutes
Serves 4

250 g/9 oz tofu (soy curd)
1 tbsp soy sauce
Pinch each dried oregano, basil and black pepper
1 small green pepper
500 g/18 oz very ripe tomatoes
1 bunch fresh mixed herbs
2 onions
3 garlic cloves
6 tbsp olive oil
125 ml/4 fl oz/½ cup soured cream
4 litres/8 pt water
2 tsp salt
400 g/14 oz wholemeal spaghetti
10 black olives
2 tbsp snipped chives
½ tsp paprika powder
Pinch cayenne pepper

Mash the tofu with a fork and mix with the soy sauce, oregano, basil and pepper. • Quarter the green pepper, wash, remove stalk, ribs, seeds, and dip with the tomatoes into boiling water. Finely shred the pepper, peel the tomatoes and dice. • Peel the onions and the garlic, finely chop and fry in the oil until transparent. • Fry the tofu for 2 minutes and then add the peppers and tomatoes and fry for an additional 1 minute. Add the herbs. Pour the soured cream over and cook in a covered pan for 10 minutes. • Bring the salted water to the boil, and cook the spaghetti for 8 minutes. Drain and place in a warmed serving dish. • Stone the olives, chop and stir into the sauce with the chives, paprika and cayenne. Pour the sauce over the spaghetti.

Spaghetti with Kidneys

Very simple and delicious

Preparation time: 1 hour
Serves 4

400 g/14 oz lambs' kidneys
1 × 400 g/14 oz can peeled tomatoes
1 bunch parsley
1 onion
3 tbsp oil
Pinch each salt and white pepper
1 tsp plain flour
1 tbsp butter
3 tbsp dry Marsala wine
4 litres/8 pt water
2 tsp salt
400 g/14 oz spaghetti

Halve the kidneys and carefully remove skin and white centres. Soak for 30 minutes, changing the cold water several times. • Drain and chop the tomatoes. Wash and dry the parsley and finely chop. Peel the onion and slice into rings; fry in oil until transparent. Add the tomatoes, salt and pepper. Allow the sauce to thicken in an uncovered pan over medium heat. • Dry the kidneys, slice, and dust with flour. • Heat the butter in a separate pan and brown the kidneys quickly. Blend in the Marsala wine. As soon as the wine has evaporated, mix the kidneys and parsley into the tomato sauce, seasoning again. • Bring the water to the boil, and add salt and spaghetti. Cook the spaghetti for about 8 minutes, until 'al dente,' then drain in a colander and serve immediately with the kidneys.

Pasta with Lamb Ragoût

A very easy Greek speciality

Preparation time: 1 hour
Serves 4

700 g/1½ lb shoulder of lamb
2 garlic cloves
1 sprig rosemary
3 tbsp oil
25 g/1 oz butter
1 tbsp tomato purée (paste)
125 ml/4 fl oz/½ cup beef stock
Pinch each salt and freshly ground white pepper
3 litres/6 pt/12 cups water
1½ tsp salt
300 g/10 oz green noodles (fettucine verdi)

Wash, dry and cut the meat into chunks, discarding any fat or bones. Peel the garlic, wash the rosemary and chop, discarding the coarse twigs. Finely chop the garlic and rosemary needles. • Heat the oil and brown the meat on all sides over a medium heat. Pour off excess fat. Add the butter, garlic and rosemary. Stir the tomato purée (paste) into the beef stock and pour over the meat. Season the meat with salt and pepper. Cook, covered, for 45–60 minutes until meat is tender. • Bring the water to the boil and add salt and noodles. Cook until 'al dente', about 8 minutes, then strain in a colander and place in a warmed serving dish. Top with the ragoût. • A freshly-made tomato salad goes well with this.

Pasta with Rabbit Stew

Very simple

Preparation time: 1 hour
Serves 4

4 leaves sage
1 sprig rosemary
2 garlic cloves
3–4 tomatoes
1 oven-ready rabbit, weighing 1.4 kg/3¼ lb
2 tbsp oil
1 tbsp butter
1 bay leaf
Pinch salt
Pinch nutmeg
125 ml/4 fl oz/½ cup white wine
2 tbsp pine kernels
300 g/10 oz pasta spirals
3 litres/6 pt/12 cups water
1½ tsp salt

Wash and pat dry the sage and the rosemary. Peel the garlic. Skin the tomatoes and cut into chunks. Joint the rabbit into 8-10 pieces, wash, carefully discarding all splinters of bone, and pat dry. • In a large pan, heat the oil and butter together, toss the herbs, bay leaf and garlic briefly in the pan, then brown the joints of meat well on all sides, and season with salt and nutmeg. Pour the wine over and allow liquid to reduce to half in the uncovered pan, turning the rabbit joints. Add the tomatoes and pine kernels and cook, covered, for 20 minutes. • Cook the pasta in boiling water for approx. 8 minutes until 'al dente', then drain in a colander. • Remove and discard the rosemary, sage and garlic from the rabbit stew before serving with the pasta. • A green salad goes well with this.

Noodles with Veal Ragoût

An Italian speciality

Preparation time: 1½ hours
Serves 4

1 × 400 g/14 oz can peeled tomatoes
2 garlic cloves
1 sprig rosemary
500 g/1 lb 2 oz veal shoulder
50 g/2 oz lean streaky bacon
40 g/1½ oz butter
125 ml/4 fl oz/½ cup dry white wine
Pinch each salt and white pepper
100 g/4 oz button mushrooms
300 g/10 oz narrow ribbon noodles
3 litres/6 pt/12 cups water
1½ tsp salt

Drain the tomatoes, reserving the juice from the can. Peel the garlic and chop finely with the rosemary. Wash the meat, dry, and make slits in it to fill with the garlic and rosemary mixture. • Finely dice the bacon and fry in 25 g/1 oz butter, until the fat runs. Brown the veal well. Pour the wine over, and boil the liquid down to half, turning the meat from time to time. Add the tomatoes to the pan and crush them with a spoon. Season the meat with salt and pepper; cook for about 1 hour, gradually adding the tomato juice. • Wash the mushrooms, dry, slice and fry in the remaining butter until the liquid has boiled off. • Cook the pasta in salted water until 'al dente'. Cut the meat into small cubes and add to the sauce with the mushrooms. Season the ragoût and serve with the pasta.

Lamb and Apple Stew with Pasta

Takes time but worth the effort

Preparation time: 2½ hours
Serves 4

700 g/1½ lb lamb taken from leg joint
2 large onions
3–4 garlic cloves
5 tbsp olive oil
Pinch each salt and black pepper
1 tsp curry powder
250 ml/8 fl oz/1 cup hot beef stock
1 bay leaf
500 g/18 oz cooking apples
3 litres/6 pt/12 cups water
1½ tsp salt
300 g/10 oz pasta (spirals or short macaroni)
1–2 tsp cornflour
3 tbsp chopped fresh parsley

Cut the meat into coarse chunks. Peel and dice the onions. Peel the garlic and chop finely. Heat 4 tbsp olive oil in a large pan and brown the meat. Add the onions and garlic and fry briefly. Season the meat with the salt, pepper and the curry powder and stir in the stock. Add the bay leaf. Cook for 1½ hours over a low heat, with the lid on. • Quarter the apples, peel, core, chop coarsely and add to the meat 20 minutes before the end of the cooking time. • Bring the water to the boil, add the salt and the remaining oil. Cook the pasta until 'al dente'. • Blend the cornflour with a little cold water and use to thicken the stew. Sprinkle the parsley over and serve with the well drained pasta.

Green Noodles with Prawns

An elegant dish

Preparation time: 30 minutes
Serves 4

300 g/10 oz peeled prawns
1 tbsp lemon juice
1 small onion
2 garlic cloves
40 g/1½ oz butter
150 ml/5 fl oz/⅔ cup double (thick) cream
175 ml/6 fl oz/¾ cup soured cream
100 g/4 oz/1 cup freshly grated Parmesan cheese
4 litres/8 pt water
3 tsp salt
1 tbsp oil
400 g/14 oz green noodles
Pinch each salt and white pepper
1 tsp dried tarragon

Rinse the prawns under cold water in a colander, drain and sprinkle with lemon juice. Peel and finely chop the onion. Peel and crush the garlic. • Heat the butter in a large pan, and briefly fry the prawns. Add the diced onion and garlic and fry lightly. Pour the cream and soured cream over the prawns and bring to the boil. Add half the Parmesan, and leave the prawns to cook over a low heat for 5 minutes. • Bring the water to the boil, add salt, oil and pasta. Cook pasta until 'al dente', then leave to drain well. Season the creamy prawn sauce with salt, pepper and tarragon, and serve with the Parmesan to accompany the pasta.

Spaghetti with Breast of Chicken

Very simple and inexpensive

Preparation time: 40 minutes
Serves 4

2 onions
500 g/1 lb 2 oz chicken breasts
200 g/7 oz/¾ cup canned sweetcorn
2 tbsp corn oil
250 ml/8 fl oz/1 cup chicken stock
Pinch each salt and cayenne pepper
4 litres/8 pt water
2 tsp salt
400 g/14 oz spaghetti
3 tbsp snipped fresh chives

Peel the onions and finely dice. Wash and dry the meat, discard skin and bones, and cut evenly into small pieces. Drain the sweetcorn. • Heat 1 tbsp of oil and fry the onions until golden. Then fry the chicken until browned. Stir in the corn, the chicken stock with salt and cayenne pepper, and cook gently over a low heat for 15 minutes. • Bring the water to a boil, adding salt and remaining oil. Cook spaghetti for about 8 minutes, until 'al dente'. • Place the well-drained pasta in a preheated serving dish, and spoon the chicken over the spaghetti, mix together and sprinkle with chives before serving.

Tip: Try adding 3 tbsp soured cream to the stew for a richer dish.

Tortellini with Chervil and Cheese Sauce

Quick and simple

Preparation time: 30 minutes
Serves 4–6

4 litres/8 pt water
2 tsp salt
1 tbsp oil
500 g/18 oz fresh tortellini stuffed with meat
1 onion
2 tbsp butter
1 heaped tbsp plain flour
125 ml/4 fl oz/½ cup hot beef stock
125 ml/4 fl oz/½ cup dry white wine
250 ml/8 fl oz/1 cup soured cream
Pinch each salt and white pepper
Pinch freshly grated nutmeg
200 g/7 oz Mozzarella cheese
1 bunch chervil
1 egg yolk

Bring the water to the boil, and add salt and oil. Cook the tortellini for about 10 minutes. Peel and finely chop the onion. • Melt the butter. Fry the chopped onion, stir in the flour and fry until golden, then gradually add the stock. Bring the sauce to the boil, stirring constantly. • Add the wine and soured cream and heat further. Season the sauce with salt, pepper and nutmeg. Place the Mozzarella cheese in the sauce in small pieces over a low heat, and allow to melt. Wash the chervil, discard coarse stems, chop roughly, and stir into the sauce. • Beat the egg yolk with 2 tbsp of sauce, and blend into the rest of the sauce. • Drain the tortellini well and mix into the sauce.

Pasta with Fennel Sauce

Quick and easy

Preparation time: 30 minutes
Serves 4

1 bulb fennel
2 sticks celery
1 green pepper
250 ml/8 fl oz/1 cup each dry white wine and instant vegetable stock
125 ml/4 fl oz/½ cup soured cream
1 tsp arrowroot (or cornflour)
Pinch each salt and white pepper
1 tsp soy sauce
4 litres/8 pt water
2 tsp salt
400 g/14 oz pasta of your choice, e.g. twists, pipes, or rigatoni
1 tbsp chopped fresh parsley

Cut the root end and the green leaves off the bulb of fennel, retaining the green parts. Remove the hard white bits from the outside, wash the fennel bulb, slice, then cut into narrow strips. Trim and clean the celery sticks, set the tender leaves aside, wash, dry and cut into very thin slices. • Halve the green pepper, discarding the core, white ribs and seeds. Dice the flesh. • Bring the wine to the boil with the vegetable stock and simmer the prepared vegetables for 10 minutes. • Blend soured cream with the arrowroot or cornflour, salt, pepper and soy sauce and thicken the sauce. • Bring the salted water to the boil, and cook the pasta according to the instructions on the packet. Wash some of the green parts of fennel and celery leaves, dry, finely chop and sprinkle over the prepared sauce with the parsley. • Serve the sauce with the cooked, drained noodles.

Penne with Creamed Artichokes

Quick and tasty

Preparation time: 20 minutes
Serves 4

4 litres/8 pt water
2 tsp salt
3 tbsp olive oil
400 g/14 oz penne
200 g/7 oz canned artichoke hearts
200 g/7 oz cream cheese
1–2 pinches white pepper

Bring the water to the boil, and add salt and 1 tsp olive oil. Cook the pasta in the boiling water for about 8 minutes until 'al dente'. • Pass the artichokes through a sieve; soften the cheese and then beat until smooth and creamy. Slowly blend in the rest of the oil and season the cream cheese with salt and pepper. Mix in the artichoke purée. Gradually stir some of the pasta cooking water into the creamy cheese sauce. • Drain the pasta in a colander, and mix well with the creamy sauce in a preheated serving dish.

Homemade Pasta with Ragoût of Duck

A special occasion meal

Preparation time: 1¾ hours
Serves 4

400 g/14 oz/3½ cups plain strong white flour
4 eggs
Pinch salt
1 onion
1 carrot
1 stick celery
1 bunch parsley

4 sage leaves

4 sprigs basil

75 g/3 oz cooked ham

500 g/18 oz very ripe tomatoes

1 small oven-ready duck

3 tbsp olive oil

250 ml/8 fl oz/1 cup dry red wine

1 bay leaf

2 cloves

Pinch each salt and freshly ground black pepper

4 litres/8 pt water

2 tsp salt

1 duck liver or 50 g/2 oz chicken livers

1 tsp butter

Using the flour, eggs and salt, prepare a pasta dough (pages 8 and 9) and leave to rest for 1 hour. • Peel the onion, scrape the carrot, clean the stick of celery; cut the vegetables into rings. Finely chop the herbs and the ham. Peel the tomatoes and cut into chunks. • Joint the duck into 8 or 10 pieces, wash and dry. Brown the vegetables, herbs, ham and duck pieces in the oil for 10 minutes, turning. Pour in the wine and cook until reduced by two thirds. • Add the tomatoes, bay leaf, cloves, salt and pepper and simmer for about 50 minutes until duck is tender. • Roll out the pasta dough thinly on a floured board, roll up like a Swiss roll, and cut into strips 1 cm/⅓ in wide. Cook the pasta in boiling water for about 4 minutes. • Cut the liver into pieces and brown in the butter, then mix into the ragoût. • Serve the noodles with the duck ragoût.

Spaghetti with Soy Sauce

A great lunch or supper dish

Preparation time: 20 minutes
Serves 4

4 litres/8 pt water
1 tsp salt
1 tbsp oil
400 g/14 oz wholewheat spaghetti or macaroni
175 g/6 oz canned bean sprouts
125 ml/4 oz/½ cup hot vegetable stock
4 tbsp soy sauce
100 g/4 oz soft tofu (bean curd)
2 tbsp soured cream
Pinch each salt and white pepper
1 tbsp chopped fresh parsley

Bring the water to the boil, adding the salt and oil. Cook the spaghetti, stirring thoroughly once, for about 10 minutes, or until 'al dente'. • Drain the bean sprouts, mix the vegetable stock with the soy sauce, tofu, soured cream, salt and pepper to taste. • Drain the spaghetti in a colander, reserving some of the cooking liquid. • Stir this liquid into the soy sauce mixture with the bean sprouts, to make a thick sauce. • Place the spaghetti in a heated dish, pour the sauce over and serve garnished with chopped parsley.

Tip: If liked, use fresh bean sprouts. Cook in the vegetable stock for 3 minutes.

Spirals with Sesame Sauce

A complete meal in itself

Preparation time: 30 minutes
Serves 4

4 litres/8 pt water
2 tsp salt
1 tbsp oil
400 g/14 oz wholemeal pasta spirals
3 garlic cloves
2 large onions
4 tbsp vegetable oil
250 ml/8 fl oz/1 cup soured cream
2 pinches mixed herbs
2 tbsp chopped fresh basil
5 tbsp sesame seeds

Bring the salted water and the oil to the boil and cook the pasta, stirring once, for about 8 minutes, until 'al dente'. • Peel the cloves of garlic and onions and finely dice. • Heat the oil in a large pan and fry the onions and garlic, stirring constantly, until transparent. Stir in the soured cream, season with the mixed herbs, and heat gently, stirring constantly. • Drain the spirals in a colander. Mix the basil and sesame seeds into the sauce. • Serve the well-drained noodles in a heated serving dish with the sauce poured over.

Ratatouille with Pasta

Healthy and delicious

Preparation time: 45 minutes
Serves 4

1 aubergine (eggplant) (approx. 250 g/9 oz)	
250 g/9 oz green pepper	
300 g/10 oz courgettes (zucchini)	
2 large onions	
3 garlic cloves	
4 tbsp olive oil	
½ vegetable stock cube	
1 tsp paprika	
Pinch cayenne	
1 tsp mixed herbs	
1 tbsp finely chopped basil	
500 g/18 oz tomatoes	
250 g/9 oz wholemeal pasta spirals	
2.5 litres/5 pt/10 cups water	
1 tsp salt	
2 tbsp snipped chives	

Peel the aubergine (eggplant), wash and cube. Quarter the green peppers, clean, wash and slice lengthways, discarding white stalky bits and seeds. Wash the courgettes (zucchini) and roughly chop. • Peel and finely chop the onions and garlic and fry in the oil in a large pan over a low heat until transparent. Add the vegetables to the onions, sprinkle in the vegetable stock powder, spices and herbs (reserve half the basil), and cook for 15 minutes. • Slit around the skins of the tomatoes, briefly dip in boiling water and peel; coarsely chop tomatoes and add to the vegetables. Cook for an additional 5 minutes. • Boil the pasta in salted water for about 8 minutes until just firm to the bite, drain in a colander. • Mix the pasta, remaining basil, and the chives with the vegetables.

Wholewheat Pasta with Spicy Stew

Nourishing and tasty

Preparation time: 45 minutes
Serves 4

250 g/9 oz green peppers	
2 onions	
3 garlic cloves	
6 tbsp olive oil	
500 g/18 oz each courgettes (zucchini) and tomatoes	
½ vegetable stock cube	
Pinch freshly ground black pepper	
250 g/9 oz wholewheat pasta spirals	
2.5 litres/5 pts/10 cups water	
1 tsp salt	
4 Frankfurter sausages	
2 tsp oregano	
2 tsp paprika	
3 tbsp snipped chives	

Quarter, trim, wash and finely slice the peppers. Peel and finely chop the onions and garlic; heat oil and gently fry onions, garlic and pepper strips over a low heat. Trim, wash, dice the courgettes (zucchini) and add to the peppers. Chop the tomatoes, discarding the stalky centres. Add the tomatoes with the stock cube and the pepper to the vegetables and cook it all together over a lower heat for 15 minutes. • Cook the pasta in boiling salted water for about 8 minutes until firm to the bite; leave to drain in a colander. • Cut the sausages into thin slices, and mix into the vegetable stew with the paprika and the oregano. Leave to cook for 5 minutes longer. Serve the stew on top of the drained spirals, garnished with the chives.

Homemade Pasta with Bacon

Easy but time consuming

Preparation time: 45 minutes
Resting time: 1 hour
Serves 4

250 g/8 oz/1¼ cups cottage cheese or ricotta
550 g/1¼ lb/5 cups plain strong white flour
4 eggs
2½ tsp salt
4 litres/8 pt water
1 tbsp oil
175 g/6 oz lean streaky bacon
2 tbsp pork dripping
150 ml/5 fl oz/⅔ cup soured cream
1–2 pinches freshly ground black pepper

Drain the cheese in a sieve and set aside. Sift the flour onto a board, and make a hollow in the middle. Add the eggs, ½ tsp salt, and then gradually add 1–2 tbsp water. Knead to a firm dough, and leave to rest for 1 hour, covered. • Thinly roll out the dough, cut into 1 cm/⅓ in strips and then into 1 cm/⅓ in squares. • Bring the water to the boil, adding the salt and the oil. Cook the pasta squares in the fast boiling water for about 3 minutes and leave to drain in a colander. • Dice the bacon and fry until crisp. Heat the pork dripping in a pan and turn the pasta in it to keep warm. Turn the pasta squares into a heated serving dish and sprinkle with the cottage or ricotta cheese. Warm the soured cream in a small saucepan, but do not allow to boil. Stir into the pasta with the bacon, season with pepper and serve.

Pasta with Viennese Liver

An Austrian speciality

Preparation time: 30 minutes
Serves 4

400 g/14 oz calves' liver
1 large onion
2 carrots
2 tbsp oil
125 ml/4 fl oz/½ cup hot beef stock
1 tbsp tomato purée (paste)
1 tsp cornflour
4 tbsp red wine
Pinch salt
½ tsp freshly ground black pepper
Pinch dried marjoram
3 litres/6 pt/12 cups water
1½ tsp salt
150 g/5 oz pasta (shells, pipes or spirals)

Cut the liver into narrow strips with a sharp knife. Peel and finely chop the onion. Scrape the carrots, wash, dry and cut into julienne strips. • Heat the oil and fry the onion until transparent. Add the liver and stir until it loses its pinkness. Pour in the stock, add the carrot slices and cook over a low heat for 5 minutes. • Mix the tomato purée with the cornflour and red wine, stir into mixture and cook until thickened. Season with salt, pepper and marjoram. • Bring the salted water to the boil, and cook the pasta until 'al dente'. Drain the pasta and serve in a warmed dish, with the liver mixture on top.

Pasta with Ham

Inexpensive and very easy

Preparation time: 30 minutes
Serves 4

200 g/7 oz cooked lean ham
40 g/1½ oz butter
1 tbsp plain flour
500 ml/1 pt hot chicken stock
1 hard-boiled egg
1 tbsp lemon juice
2 tbsp soured cream
½ bunch parsley
4 litres/8 pt water
2 tsp salt
1 tbsp oil
200 g/7 oz pasta (shells, pipes, or spirals)

Dice the ham. Melt the butter in a saucepan and cook the flour until golden. Stir and add the chicken stock gradually. Let the sauce cook gently for a few minutes, stirring occasionally. • Chop the hard-boiled egg and mix into the sauce with the lemon juice and ham. Stir in the soured cream. • Rinse the parsley under the cold tap, pat dry, finely chop and stir into the sauce. • Bring the water to the boil, add salt and oil, and cook the pasta until 'al dente'. • Let the cooked pasta drain in a colander, and serve immediately with the ham sauce.

Tip: Diced leftover chicken or turkey may be used in place of the ham, and 1 tbsp of capers may be used to garnish the dish.

Spätzle with Emmental Cheese

A classic recipe

Preparation time: 45 minutes
Serves 4

150 g/5 oz Emmental cheese
2 large onions
375 g/12 oz/3 cups strong plain white flour
125 ml/4 fl oz/½ cups water
2 eggs
2½ tsp salt
4 litres/8 pt water
50 g/2 oz butter

Grate the cheese. Peel the onions and cut into thin rings. • Sift the flour into a bowl, add water, eggs and ½ tsp salt and work quickly to a soft but not runny dough. Add either more water or flour as required. • Bring the water to the boil with the remaining salt. Work small pieces of the dough back and forth on a dampened board, stretching and pulling, and then cut the dough into narrow strips with a long knife and place in boiling water. Alternatively, the spätzle may be pushed through a coarse sieve or through a special spätzle machine. They are cooked when they float to the surface. • Remove with a slotted spoon and leave to drain in a colander. Keep warm. • Melt the butter in a large pan and fry the onion rings until golden. Place the spätzle in a heated serving dish, and pile the cheese on top. Garnish with the onion rings.

Pasta with White Cabbage

Unusual and nourishing

Preparation time: 1¾ hours
Serves 4

250 g/9 oz/2¼ cups strong plain white flour
2 eggs
Pinch salt
1 onion
1 small head white cabbage (approx. 500 g/1 lb 2 oz)
3 tbsp pork dripping or lard
1 tbsp sugar
125 ml/4 fl oz/½ cup hot vegetable stock
Pinch each salt and freshly ground black pepper
3 litres/6 pt/12 cups water
1½ tsp salt
1 tbsp oil

Work the flour, eggs, salt and enough water to make a pliable dough. Leave to rest under an inverted bowl for 1 hour. • Peel the onion and cut into thin rings. Remove the outside leaves from the white cabbage and discard. Cut cabbage into four parts, wash, and finely shred, discarding the stalk. • Melt the dripping or lard and fry the onion rings until golden, sprinkle the sugar over, and leave to caramelise in the pan. Add the shredded cabbage, briefly fry, pour the stock over, and season with salt and pepper. Cook, covered, for 30 minutes. • Thinly roll out the dough on a floured board, and cut into 4 cm/½ in squares and leave to dry for a few minutes. • Bring the water to the boil, add the salt and the oil, and cook the squares for about 4 minutes, then drain in a colander. Mix into the cabbage and leave in a warm place for a few minutes before serving.

Rye Spätzle with Tomato Sauce

A wholemeal recipe

Preparation time: 1¼ hours
Serves 4

175 g/6 oz/1½ cups each wheatmeal flour and rye flour
½ tsp ground caraway
Pinch each sea salt and black pepper
120 g/4 oz/1 cup grated Parmesan cheese
5 eggs
1 large onion
1 garlic clove
3 tbsp olive oil
350 ml/12 fl oz/1½ cups water
1 can tomato purée (paste) (70 g/2½ oz)
1 tbsp wheatmeal flour
1 tsp mixed dried herbs
5 tbsp single (light) cream
1–2 pinches each sea salt and black pepper
Pinch sugar
½–1 tsp paprika
2 tbsp snipped chives
3 litres/6 pt/12 cups water
1½ tsp salt

Make a soft spätzle dough from the 2 flours, caraway, salt, pepper, 60 g/2 oz/½ cup Parmesan, eggs and about 4 tbsp water and leave to rest for 30 minutes. • Peel the onion and garlic and chop finely; fry in oil until transparent. Mix the water with the tomato purée (paste), flour and herbs, pour over the onions and cook for 5 minutes, stirring. Remove the pan from the heat and stir in an additional 25 g/1 oz/¼ cup Parmesan and cream. Stir in salt, pepper, sugar and paprika and turn into a large warmed serving dish. • Shape the spätzle on a dampened wooden board, in batches, and cook in boiling salted water for 1 minute. Scoop them out with a spoon, briefly drain, and add to the tomato sauce. • Serve garnished with the remaining Parmesan and chives.

Fettucine with Herb Purée and Vegetables

Very simple

Preparation time: 1 hour
Serves 4

4 onions
250 g/9 oz courgettes (zucchini)
2 green peppers
250 g/9 oz mushrooms
3 tomatoes
7 tbsp olive oil
¼ chicken stock cube
Pinch black pepper
2 sprigs tarragon
1 bunch each parsley, dill and basil
6 sage leaves
2 garlic cloves
2 tbsp flaked almonds
Pinch each salt and freshly ground black pepper
1 tbsp lemon juice
350 g/12 oz fettucine (tagliatelle)
3 litres/6 pt/12 cups water
1½ tsp salt

Peel the onions, cut in half downwards and into strips. Wash the courgettes (zucchini), halve and slice. Clean and shred the peppers. Wash the mushrooms, and halve if large. Peel and dice the tomatoes, discarding the seeds and stalky centre. • Heat 4 tbsp olive oil. First, fry the onions until transparent, and then add the courgettes (zucchini), peppers and mushrooms and cook 5 minutes longer. • Sprinkle with the stock cube and the pepper, and cook, covered, for 10 minutes over a low heat. • Wash and pat the herbs dry, remove coarse stems, and chop. Peel the garlic and crush through a press. Mix with the crumbled flaked almonds and the herbs. Add the salt, pepper, lemon juice and remaining oil. • Stir the tomatoes into the vegetables, and simmer to allow liquid to evaporate a little. • Cook the pasta in salted water for 8 minutes until firm to the bite, then drain. Serve with the vegetables and the herb purée.

Tarhonya with Creamy Mushroom Sauce

An Hungarian speciality

Drying time: 14 hours
Preparation time: 45 minutes
Serves 4

2 eggs

Pinch salt

250 g/9 oz/2¼ cups strong plain white flour (approx.)

2 small onions

8 tbsp sunflower oil

½ tsp salt

1 tsp paprika

250 g/9 oz button mushrooms

1 tbsp plain flour

A few drops lemon juice

Pinch black pepper

250 ml/8 fl oz/1 cup soured cream

2 tbsp chopped fresh parsley

Mix the eggs and salt in a bowl, and add as much flour as needed to make a very firm dough. Leave the dough to dry for 2 hours, then coarsely grate and spread out to dry overnight. • Peel and finely chop the onions. Fry half in 5 tbsp oil. Toss the "pasta pearls" in the oil and cover with water, season with salt and paprika and cook for about 6 minutes; if necessary, add more water. Just before the end of the cooking time, turn the "pasta pearls" and allow to separate in the open pan. • Clean, wash and slice the mushrooms, and fry with the remaining onions in the rest of the oil until the juices have evaporated. Add 1 tbsp flour and about 2 tbsp water. Flavour with the lemon juice, and a little salt and pepper. Stir in the soured cream and parsley and cook for a few minutes longer. • Serve with the "pasta pearls."

Spirals with Aubergines (Eggplants)

Inexpensive and simple

Preparation time: 1 hour
Serves 4

2 garlic cloves

4 very ripe tomatoes

2 small aubergines (eggplants)

2 yellow peppers

100 g/4 oz/¾ cup green olives

1 bunch basil

2 anchovy fillets

1 tbsp capers

4–5 tbsp olive oil

125 ml/4 fl oz/½ cup hot chicken stock

½ tsp each salt and pepper

400 g/14 oz pasta spirals (or substitute spaghetti or fusilli)

4 litres/8 pt water

2 tsp salt

Peel the garlic and crush flat. Skin the tomatoes, discarding the central stalks, and chop the flesh into chunks. Wash the aubergines (eggplants), dry and dice. Quarter the peppers, clean, dry, and slice finely. Stone and coarsely chop the olives. Wash and pat dry basil, and chop finely with the anchovy fillets and capers. • Heat the oil, fry the garlic until brown, then discard the garlic. Fry the diced aubergines (eggplants), then add the tomatoes, the pepper strips, the anchovies, capers, olives, basil and chicken stock. Leave the mixture to thicken for 30 minutes, adding more stock if needed, and season with salt and pepper. • Cook the pasta until 'al dente' in boiling salted water, then drain and mix in a warmed serving dish with the vegetables.

Pasta with Bean Sprouts

A speciality from Singapore

Preparation time: 30 minutes
Serves 4

3 litres/6 pt/12 cups water
1½ tsp salt
1 tbsp oil
300 g/10 oz vermicelli
175 g/6 oz bean sprouts
2 fresh chilli peppers
2 spring onions
25 g/1 oz fresh root ginger
300 g/10 oz pork fillet
3 tbsp each sesame seed oil and soy sauce
Pinch each salt and freshly ground white pepper

Bring the salted water and oil to the boil, and shake the vermicelli into the boiling water, stir once and cook for 4 minutes. Drain the pasta. • Rinse and drain the bean sprouts in a colander. Clean, wash, dry and cut the chilli peppers and spring onions into rings. Peel and finely chop the ginger. Wash, dry and cut the pork fillet into about 6 mm/¼ in strips. • Heat the oil in a wok or a large pan and fry the ginger, stirring constantly. Add the meat and cook for 2 minutes. Add bean sprouts, chillies and spring onions and stir-fry for 3 minutes. • Finally, stir in the well-drained pasta and cook for 3 minutes. Season the pasta with soy sauce, salt and pepper. • Serve with soy sauce.

Glass Noodles with Prawns

Exotic and delicate

Preparation time: 1 hour
Serves 4

200 g/7 oz glass noodles (transparent)
400 g/14 oz onions
1 small red pepper
3 garlic cloves
250 g/9 oz pork fillet
3 tbsp corn oil
350 g/12 oz bean sprouts
3 tbsp soy sauce
2 tbsp oyster sauce
Pinch salt
2–3 tbsp sugar
Juice from ½ lemon
250 g/8 oz cooked prawns
2 tbsp chopped parsley or 1 tsp chopped coriander
Oil, for deep frying

With scissors, cut the glass noodles into pieces about 7.5 cm/3 in length. Heat the oil to 180°C/350°F in a deep fryer and deep fry the noodles in batches until golden. Lift from oil with draining spoon and leave to drain. • Peel the onions and cut into rings. Halve the red pepper, remove stalky part and seeds, and dice finely with the peeled garlic. Cut the pork fillet into strips about 1 cm/⅓ in thick, heat the corn oil and fry the pork for 2 minutes, turning constantly; remove from the oil. • Sauté the onion rings, garlic and pepper pieces in the oil for 2 minutes. Add the bean sprouts, soy and oyster sauces, salt, sugar and lemon juice. Stir-fry for another 5 minutes. • Mix the pasta, the meat and the prawns together and heat. Garnish with parsley.

Noodles with Chicken and Prawns

Oriental speciality

Preparation time: 45 minutes
Serves 4

225 g/8 oz egg noodles (or thin spaghetti)

3 litres/6 pt/12 cups water

1½ tsp salt

300 g/10 oz chicken breast fillets

250 g/9 oz Chinese leaves

4 spring onions

3 sticks celery

1 small red pepper

2 garlic cloves

4 tbsp oil

250 g/9 oz prawns

125 ml/4 fl oz/½ cup chicken stock

2 tbsp soy sauce

3 tsp chopped fresh root ginger

Cook the noodles (or spaghetti) in boiling salted water according to packet instructions. Drain and set aside. • Wash, dry and slice the chicken breast fillets into strips 1 cm/⅓ in thick. • Trim the Chinese leaves, rinse, pat dry and shred. Trim the spring onions and slice finely. Wash and dry the celery, remove coarse threads and then slice finely. Wash the pepper, dry, halve and remove seeds and dice. Peel and finely chop the garlic. • Heat 2 tbsp of the oil in a large frying pan or wok and fry the garlic for 30 seconds until softened, but not brown. Add the chicken and stir-fry for about 2 minutes. • Add the stock, soy sauce and seasoning and simmer until reduced by a third. Remove from the pan and set aside. • Heat the remaining oil in the pan, add the ginger, spring onions, celery and pepper and stir-fry for 2 minutes. Add the prawns and Chinese leaves and stir-fry until heated through. Add the chicken, stock and noodles and heat through before serving.

Noodles with Horseradish

A Japanese speciality

Preparation time: 40 minutes
Serves 4

4 litres/8 pt water
1 tsp salt
400 g/14 oz Udon (Japanese pasta)
3 onions
250 g/9 oz button mushrooms
250 g/9 oz carrots
4 tbsp oil
250 g/9 oz prawns
4 tbsp soy sauce
4 tbsp sweet and sour sauce
4 tbsp grated white horseradish

Bring the salted water to the boil and cook the pasta for about 8 minutes until firm to the bite, then drain in a colander. • Peel and finely chop the onions. Clean the mushrooms and slice. Scrape the carrots under warm running water, dry and grate. • Heat the oil in a large pan and fry the chopped onions. Add the mushrooms and carrots and stir-fry for 3 minutes. • Mix in the prawns, soy sauce, sweet and sour sauce and the cooked pasta. Keep warm over a very low heat. • Serve the pasta with the grated white horseradish.

Chickpea Pasta with Curry Sauce

Exotic and delicious

Preparation time: 2 hours
Serves 4

185 g/6 oz/1 cup Besan (chickpea flour, or substitute pea-flour from yellow peas)
1 tsp baking powder
2 tbsp oil
8-9 tbsp water
½ tsp salt
Pinch cayenne pepper
4 onions
2 apples
500 g/1 lb 2 oz lamb
50 g/2 oz butter
2 heaped tbsp curry powder
2 firm bananas
250 ml/8 fl oz/1 cup soured cream
Oil for deep frying

Work the chickpea flour, baking powder, oil, water, salt and cayenne pepper into a dough, and leave covered for 1 hour. • Peel and dice the onions and apples. Cut the lamb into 2.5 cm/1 in pieces. Melt the butter in a large frying pan, and brown the meat on all sides for 2 minutes, add the onions and apples, season and cook for 5 minutes more. Mix the curry powder into the sauce and simmer, covered, over a low heat for 30 minutes. • Peel and slice the bananas, and mix into the sauce with soured cream. Gently cook for another 30 minutes. • Thinly roll out the pasta dough on a floured workboard, and cut into thin strips. • Heat the oil to 180°C/350°F and deep-fry the pasta in batches until golden. Drain and serve with curry sauce.

Chow Mein

A Chinese speciality

Preparation time: 1 hour
Serves 4

12 black dried mushrooms (Mu Err)
3 litres/6 pt/12 cups water
1½ tsp salt
300 g/10 oz Chinese egg noodles
400 g/14 oz pork fillet
1–2 tbsp cornflour
3 tbsp soy sauce
2 spring onions
2 carrots
250 g/9 oz bean sprouts
4 tbsp corn oil
Oil for deep frying

Leave the dried mushrooms to soak covered with lukewarm water. • Bring the salted water to the boil and cook the egg noodles for 6 minutes, then shake in a colander, rinse with cold water and dry on paper towels. • Cut the pork fillet into thin strips. First dip into the cornflour and then turn in 1 tbsp soy sauce. • Trim the onions and cut into rings. Scrape and wash the carrots, dry and cut into thin slices. • Heat the oil in a deep fryer to 180°C/350°F. Fry the pasta in portions until crispy and brown, then drain on absorbent paper, and keep warm. • Heat the corn oil in a pan and fry the meat, stirring, for 2 minutes. Add the carrots, the onion rings, and the rinsed, drained bean sprouts; stir-fry together for 3 minutes more. • Add the mushrooms with the soaking liquid and the remaining soy sauce to the meat, and cook together for 2 minutes. Season with salt, and thicken gradually with 1 tsp of cornflour, blended with some soy sauce. • Serve with the noodles.

Beef Olives with Glass Noodles

A Vietnamese speciality

Preparation time: 1½ hours
Serves 4

450 g/1 lb fillet steak
2 garlic cloves
2 tbsp cornflour
2 tbsp each soy sauce and medium-dry sherry
Pinch each salt, white pepper and Chinese 5-spice powder
3 tbsp oil
225 g/8 oz glass (transparent) noodles
4 spring onions
1 litre/2 pt/5 cups water
Juice of 1 lemon
125 ml/4 fl oz/½ cup each soy sauce and sherry
16 lettuce leaves
16 slices cucumber

Trim meat and cut into 16 thin slices. Peel garlic and crush through garlic press, and mix with cornflour, soy sauce, sherry, salt, pepper, Chinese 5-spice powder and 2 tbsp oil. Coat the slices of meat on both sides with the mixture and leave to marinate for 1 hour. • Pour cold water over the glass noodles and leave to soften for 10 minutes. • Trim the spring onions, wash and cut into thin slices. • Cover the marinated slices of fillet with the spring onion, roll up and secure on wooden skewers. • Bring the water to the boil. Dip the pasta in for 1 minute, drain in a colander. • Heat the remaining oil in a pan, stir in noodles and keep warm over a low heat. Place the skewered meat on a grill and cook for 5–7 minutes, turning frequently. • Mix the lemon juice with the soy sauce and sherry, and turn into 4 side bowls. • Arrange the lettuce, cucumber slices and pasta on 4 plates, and put the skewers on top of the salad. To eat, wrap the meat and pasta in lettuce leaves and dip into the sauce.

Glass Noodles with Egg Sauce

A Chinese speciality

Preparation time: 30 minutes
Serves 4

8 dried black mushrooms (Mu Err)	
300 g/10 oz glass (transparent) noodles	
450 g/1 lb pork fillet	
4 spring onions	
4 tbsp oil	
½ tsp salt	
2 tbsp well-flavoured hot chicken stock	
6 tbsp dry sherry	
4 tbsp soy sauce	
3 litres/6 pt/12 cups water	
4 egg yolks	

Cover the mushrooms with lukewarm water, and leave to soak. Cut the glass noodles into pieces about 5 cm/2 in long with scissors and soften in cold water for 10 minutes. • Cut the pork fillet into thin strips. Trim the spring onions, wash thoroughly, dry and cut into thin rings. • Heat the oil. Stir-fry the meat for 2 minutes, and season. Add the rings of spring onions, the stock, sherry, soy sauce and mushrooms with the soaking water to the meat mixture, bring to the boil and cook for 1 minute. • Bring the water to the boil and cook the noodles for 1 minute, drain well and arrange on 4 warmed dishes. Beat the egg yolks and pour over the noodles. Spoon the piping hot meat sauce over each serving of noodles.

Rice Noodles with Beef

A special dish

Preparation time: 1 hour 15 minutes
Serves 4

300 g/10 oz wide rice noodles	
450 g/1 lb rump steak	
2 tbsp soy sauce	
2 tbsp sake (rice wine)	
1 tbsp cornflour	
4 spring onions	
250 g/9 oz mushrooms	
3 litres/6 pt/12 cups water	
5 tbsp oil	
250 g/9 oz bean sprouts	
1 tsp salt	
2 tsp sugar	
3 tbsp white wine vinegar	
Pinch freshly ground black pepper	

Leave the noodles to soak for 1 hour covered in cold water. • Cut the steak into strips 1 cm/⅓ in thick. Mix the soy sauce with the rice wine, and turn the strips of meat in it. Then stir in the cornflour, cover and leave to marinate. • Wash, dry and cut the spring onions into rings. • Bring the water to the boil, and cook the noodles for 1 minute, shake in a colander, rinse with cold water and drain. • Heat the oil in a wok or high-sided pan, and fry the meat strips for 2 minutes, remove, cover and keep warm. • Fry the onion rings for 1 minute in oil, add the mushrooms and the rinsed bean sprouts, and add the rest of the salt, sugar, vinegar and pepper, and cook for 3 more minutes. • Add the noodles and the meat. Stir-fry for 2 minutes and serve.

Baked and Stuffed Pasta Dishes

Pasta Roulade with Spinach

Impressive

Preparation time: 2½ hours
Serves 6

275 g/10 oz/2½ cups plain strong white flour
2 eggs
Salt
2 tsp oil
Approx. 125 ml/4 fl oz/½ cup lukewarm water
500 g/18 oz spinach
2 shallots
1 garlic clove
40 g/1½ oz butter
Pinch white pepper
200 g/7 oz lean cooked ham, thinly sliced
250 g/9 oz/1¼ cups ricotta
125 ml/4 fl oz/½ cup soured cream
200 g/7 oz Mozzarella cheese
½ bunch parsley
Pinch grated nutmeg
4 litres/8 pt water
500 g/18 oz tomatoes
Pinch each dried thyme and basil
50 g/2 oz/½ cup freshly grated Parmesan cheese
Butter for the cooking dish

Mix the flour with the eggs, a pinch of salt, 1 tsp oil and as much water as needed to form a smooth shiny dough. Shape the dough into a large sausage-shape, brush with remaining oil and leave to rest under an inverted dish for 1 hour. • Wash the spinach thoroughly, remove tough stems and cook in a large pan for 2–3 minutes or until leaves are wilted. Drain well. • Peel shallots and garlic, finely chop and mix with butter, pepper, a good pinch of salt and the spinach. • Dice the ham, and mix with the ricotta and soured cream. Dice the Mozzarella. Chop the parsley and add to the cream mixture with half the Mozzarella, nutmeg, salt and pepper. • Roll out the pasta dough into a rectangle measuring 50 × 35.5 cm/20 × 14 in on a tea towel. Spread with the cream and ham mixture and then the spinach mixture. Roll up the dough, using the tea towel, dab the ends of the roll with water, and firmly shape into a circle. • Place the pasta roll in a very large saucepan, and cook uncovered in boiling water for about 30 minutes. • Slit the tomatoes around the bottoms, place in boiling water, peel, discard the central stalky parts and sauté with the herbs until the liquid almost vanishes. Then mix with the remaining Mozzarella. •

Heat the oven to 230°C/450°F/Gas Mark 8, and butter a round 25 cm/10 in ovenproof dish. Carefully place the pasta roll into the oven dish, cover with tomato sauce, sprinkle with Parmesan and bake for 15 minutes.

Tip: Swiss chard could be used if available. Remove tough stalks, cut into strips and blanch in boiling water for 2 minutes. Drain and use as for spinach. The leftover roulade can be re-heated well. Cut it into thick slices, dot with butter and Parmesan, and bake in a preheated 220°C/425°F/Gas Mark 7 oven for 10 minutes.

Classic Cannelloni

An Italian speciality

Preparation time: 1 hour
Baking time: 45 minutes
Serves 4

1 large onion
2 garlic cloves
2 tbsp olive oil
250 g/9 oz minced beef
Salt and freshly ground black pepper
½ tsp each dried oregano and sage
2 tsp tomato purée (paste)
400 g/14 oz canned peeled tomatoes
250 g/9 oz cannelloni
2.5 litres/5 pt/10 cups water
150 g/5 oz/1¼ cups grated Parmesan cheese
3 tbsp soured cream
50 g/2 oz butter

Heat the oven to 200°C/ 400°F/Gas Mark 6. Peel and finely chop the onion and garlic, brown in oil with the minced beef for a few minutes. • Remove from heat, season with salt, pepper, herbs and tomato purée (paste), and leave to cool. • Crush the tomatoes, heat with the juice, uncovered, until some of the liquid has evaporated. • Pre-cook the cannelloni, if necessary, in boiling salted water; drain. • Stir half the Parmesan cheese with the soured cream into the meat and fill the tubes. Arrange in an oven-proof dish. Pour the tomatoes over, sprinkle with the remaining cheese, and top with dabs of butter. • Bake the cannelloni in the oven (middle shelf) for 45 minutes. • A green salad goes very well with this.

Cannelloni with Vegetable Filling

Inexpensive and easy to make

Preparation time: 45 minutes
Baking time: 20 minutes
Serves 4

1 large Spanish onion
2 young carrots
1 small kohlrabi
2 tbsp olive oil
150 g/5 oz/1 cup frozen peas
3 tbsp chopped fresh parsley
1 tbsp each chopped fresh thyme and basil or ½ tsp each if dried
5 tbsp dry white wine
250 g/9 oz cannelloni
2.5 litres/5 pt/10 cups water
Salt
Freshly ground black pepper
125 ml/4 fl oz/½ cup soured cream
75 g/3 oz/¾ cup grated Parmesan
50 g/2 oz butter

Peel and finely chop the onion, scrape, wash and slice the carrots into julienne strips. Peel and dice the kohlrabi. Heat the oil and fry the onion until transparent. Add the prepared vegetables with the peas, the herbs and wine, and sauté for 5 minutes; leave to cool. • If necessary, pre-cook the pasta in boiling salted water. • Preheat the oven to 230°C/450°F/ Gas Mark 8. Mix the vegetables with salt, pepper, soured cream and 50 g/2 oz/½ cup Parmesan and use to fill the drained tubes. • Butter a baking dish well and lay the cannelloni in, sprinkle with the rest of the grated cheese, dot with butter and bake for 20 minutes.

Austrian Ravioli

A delicious starter or main course

Preparation time: 1¾ hours
Serves 4–6

275 g/10 oz/2½ cups plain strong white flour
4 eggs
2 pinches salt
350 g/¾ lb cooked beef
1 onion
1 bunch parsley
1 tbsp pork dripping or lard
Pinch freshly ground black pepper
Pinch each dried thyme and marjoram
1 egg white
4–5 litres/8–10 pt water
2 tsp salt

Using the flour, 3 eggs, 1 pinch salt and water as needed, make a pliable pasta dough. Leave the dough to rest for 1 hour, covered. • Put the meat through grinder or chop very finely. Peel and finely chop the onion. Wash, pat dry and chop the parsley. • Heat the dripping or lard in a pan and fry the onion until transparent, then add the meat. Mix with 1 pinch salt, pepper, thyme, marjoram and parsley. Briefly cook the meat, then mix in the remaining egg. • Roll out the dough on a floured board until 2 mm/⅛th in thick. Place teaspoons of filling on one half of dough (about 4 cm/1½ in apart) and brush between the filling with lightly beaten egg white. Fold the second half of the dough on top, and press down firmly between the spoonfuls of stuffing. Cut out four-cornered "ravioli" with a pastry wheel. • Bring the salted water to a boil in a large saucepan, and cook the pockets for about 5 minutes. • These are very good as shown here in a meat consommé, or baked in butter with a tomato sauce.

Tyrolean Stuffed Pasta

An Austrian speciality

Preparation time: 1¾ hours
Serves 4

275 g/10 oz/2½ cups plain strong white flour
3 eggs
2 pinches salt
500 g/18 oz spinach
100 g/4 oz butter
Pinch each white pepper and grated nutmeg
100 g/4 oz/1 cup grated Emmental
1 egg white
4 litres/8 pt water
2 tsp salt
6 tbsp snipped chives

Using the flour, eggs, 1 pinch salt and water as needed, make a pliable pasta dough. Leave the dough to rest for 1 hour, covered. • Wash the spinach thoroughly and cook over a moderate heat, without any added water, until wilted, then drain, squeeze well and chop finely. • Melt half the butter. Add the spinach, and season with 1 pinch salt, pepper and nutmeg. Let the liquid evaporate and the spinach cool. Mix in 50 g/2 oz Emmental cheese. • Roll out the dough and cut circles of 7.5 cm/3 in diameter. Place a teaspoon of the spinach mixture on one half of each circle, painting the edges of the dough with the beaten egg white. Press the edges together into crescent-shapes, and lay on a floured tea towel. • Bring the salted water to the boil, and cook the stuffed pasta for 6 minutes. Melt the remaining butter. • Lift the stuffed pasta from the water, pour the butter over and serve, garnished with the snipped chives and the remaining cheese.

Stuffed Pasta Crescents

An Austrian speciality

Preparation time: 1¾ hours
Serves 4

300 g/10 oz/2½ cups plain strong white flour
3 eggs
Salt
175 g/6 oz floury potatoes
275 g/10 oz/1⅓ cups ricotta
50 g/2 oz soft butter
125 ml/4 fl oz/½ cup soured cream
1 tsp each freshly chopped mint, parsley, chervil and chives
Pinch black pepper
1 egg white
4 litres/8 pt water
175 g/6 oz lean streaky bacon

Using the flour, eggs, 1 pinch salt and water as needed, make a pliable pasta dough. Shape the dough into a roll, and rest for 1 hour, covered. • Peel, wash, dice and cook the potatoes in a little salted water for 15 minutes. Mix together the ricotta, butter, soured cream and herbs and season with salt and pepper. • Drain the potatoes well and leave to cool, then press through a sieve and mix with the ricotta mixture. • Roll out the dough, in two or four batches, until 2 mm/⅛th in thick. Cut out 9 cm/3½ in circles, place a little filling on one half of each circle and fold in half, sealing the edges well with beaten egg white and fluting the edge between the thumb and finger. • Bring salted water to the boil, and cook the pasta for 5 minutes. • Chop the bacon, fry until crisp and use to garnish the well-drained pasta.

Baked Pasta Squares

A Greek speciality

Preparation time: 35 minutes
Serves 4

50 g/2 oz/⅓ cup fine semolina
5 tbsp milk
250 g/9 oz/2¼ cups plain flour
2 eggs
1 tsp salt
2 garlic cloves
1 large onion
1 stick celery
2 tomatoes
4 tbsp olive oil
Pinch each salt, black pepper and sugar
4 litres/8 pt water
2 tsp salt
2 tbsp chopped fresh parsley
100 g/4 oz/1 cup freshly grated Parmesan cheese

Mix the semolina with the milk and leave to soak for 1 hour. • Work the flour, semolina, eggs and salt together into a firm, pliable dough. Leave the dough to rest under a hot dish for 1 hour. • Roll the dough out in portions the thickness of a knife, and leave the pieces to dry for 1 hour. • Peel the garlic and onion, and dice both finely. Wash the celery, dry, discard coarse threads, and slice thinly. Peel and chop the tomatoes. • Heat the oil, and fry the onion, celery and garlic for 5 minutes, stirring. Add the pieces of tomato, season with salt, pepper and sugar and leave to simmer, stirring from time to time. • Bring the salted water to the boil, and cook the pasta for about 5 minutes, until 'al dente', then drain in a colander. Combine with the sauce and simmer together for 3 minutes. • Garnish the pasta and vegetable mixture with parsley and cheese before serving.

Banitza

A Bulgarian speciality

Preparation time: 1 hour
Baking time: 30–40 minutes
Serves 4

500 g/18 oz/4½ cups flour
2 pinches salt
1 tbsp wine vinegar
Approx. 350 ml/12 fl oz/1½ cups water
2 eggs
400 g/14 oz goat's cheese
3 tbsp soured cream
1 bunch dill
1 garlic clove
Pinch black pepper

Preheat the oven to 180°C/ 350°F/Gas Mark 4. Mix the flour with 1 pinch salt, the vinegar and as much water as the flour absorbs to a smooth dough and leave to rest under a damp tea towel for 1 hour. • Separate the yolks and whites of eggs to make the filling. Cream the cheese and mix with the egg yolks and soured cream. Wash the dill, pat dry and chop. Peel garlic, chop and crush with 1 pinch salt. Whisk the egg whites until stiff. Stir the dill, garlic, and pepper into the creamed mixture, and fold in the egg whites gently. • Oil a baking tray. Shape the dough into 10 equal balls. Roll out two balls to half the size of the baking sheet making sure to keep remaining dough covered. Lay 1 piece of dough on the baking tray, brush with oil and lay the second on top. Spread one quarter of the filling on the dough, and then proceed in the same manner with the remaining balls and the filling. Brush the last sheets of dough with oil. • Bake the Banitza in the oven for 30 to 35 minutes, and leave to rest briefly. Cut into rectangles.

Pasta with Celery

Quick and inexpensive

Preparation time: 40 minutes
Serves 4

500 g/18 oz celery
1 garlic clove
1 onion
2 tbsp oil
125 ml/4 fl oz/½ cup each vegetable stock and dry white wine
400 g/14 oz pasta of your choice, e.g. spirals, shells or penne
4 litres/8 pt water
2 tsp salt
3 tbsp sesame seeds
2 tsp arrowroot (or substitute cornflour)
3 tbsp single (light) cream
Pinch each salt and freshly ground black pepper

Remove the coarse threads from the celery sticks and cut the ends off, reserving some tender leaves for garnishing. Wash the celery sticks and slice thinly. Peel and finely chop the garlic and onion. Fry until transparent in the oil. Add the celery, pour the vegetable stock and white wine over, and leave to braise for 10 minutes. • Cook the pasta in boiling salted water until still firm to the bite, rinse under cold water in a colander and then leave to drain. • Toast the sesame seeds in a pan without oil until golden. • Blend the arrowroot or cornflour with the cream until smooth, and thicken the celery juices. Let the vegetables cook for a few more minutes, season with salt and pepper and throw in the sesame seeds. • Stir the cooked pasta into the vegetables. • Garnish with celery tops and serve with grated Emmental if liked.

Ravioli with Cheese Filling

Excellent starter

Preparation time: 1¾ hours
Serves 4–6

6–7 eggs
½ tsp salt
2 tbsp oil
500 g/18 oz/2½ cups plain strong white flour
250 g/9 oz Parmesan cheese
250 g/9 oz/1¼ cups ricotta cheese
Pinch white pepper
Pinch grated nutmeg
2–3 litres/4–6 pt/8–12 cups water
1 tsp salt (for water)
100 g/4 oz butter

To make the pasta dough, crack 4 or 5 eggs into a bowl, according to their size. Stir in the salt and oil, add some of the flour and mix to a thin dough. Sift the remaining flour into a bowl, add the egg mixture and work to a smooth pliable dough. Leave under an inverted dish to rest for 1 hour. • Grate the Parmesan and mix 150 g/5 oz/1¼ cups with the ricotta, remaining eggs, some salt, pepper and nutmeg. • Roll out the pasta dough to 2 mm/⅛th in thick on a floured work surface, or process as thinly as possible in a pasta machine, then cut into 5 cm/2 in squares. Divide the filling among the squares. Wet the edges of the squares with water and firmly fold the ravioli in half. • Bring the salted water to the boil, and cook the ravioli for 5 minutes, then lift out and leave to drain. • Melt the butter and stir-fry the ravioli very carefully. Serve sprinkled with remaining grated Parmesan.

Ravioli with Spinach Filling

An Italian speciality

Preparation time: 1¾ hours
Serves 4

275 g/10 oz/2¼ cups plain strong white flour
2 eggs
Pinch salt
3 tbsp walnut oil
125 ml/4 fl oz/½ cup lukewarm water
300 g/10 oz spinach
2 garlic cloves
100 g/4 oz finely ground steak
1–2 tbsp corn oil
100 g/4 oz Feta, crumbled
2 tbsp coarsely chopped pistachio nuts
Pinch each salt, black pepper and grated nutmeg
3 litres/6 pt/12 cups water
1 tsp each salt and oil (for water)

Using the flour, eggs, walnut oil and as much water as needed, make a pliable pasta dough. Coat the dough with oil and leave to rest for 1 hour, covered. • Wash the spinach thoroughly and cook quickly for 2 minutes, then press well and chop roughly. Peel and finely chop the garlic, crush and mix into the ground steak. Brown the steak in the corn oil, leave to cool a little and mix with spinach, Feta, pistachios and spices. Roll out the dough thinly in two portions on a floured work surface. Place the spinach mixture in small heaps on one piece of dough, paint around the heaps with water, lay the second piece of dough on top, and press down well between the filling to seal. Cut out with ravioli cutter. Add salt and oil to a pan of boiling water and cook ravioli for 5 minutes. Serve with tomato sauce.

Tortellini Filled with Prawns

Time consuming but worth the effort

Preparation time: 2 hours
Serves 4–6

300 g/10 oz/2½ cups plain strong white flour
3 eggs
Salt
4 tbsp oil
250 g/10 oz/1⅔ cups peeled prawns
2 tomatoes
3 shallots
1 tsp cornflour
3 tbsp white wine
3 tbsp soured cream
White pepper
1 tbsp lemon juice
2 tbsp chopped fresh dill
3 litres/6 pt/12 cups water
1 tsp salt and oil (for water)
40 g/1½ oz/⅓ cup grated cheddar

Using the flour, eggs, a pinch of salt and 3 tbsp oil, make a workable pasta dough and leave to rest for 1 hour, covered. • Chop the prawns. Pour boiling water over the tomatoes, peel, quarter, remove seeds and stalky parts and dice. Peel the shallots and dice. Blend the cornflour with the white wine. • Fry the shallots in the remaining oil until transparent, add the tomatoes and soured cream. Cook for 5 minutes, stirring. Add the blended cornflour, a pinch of salt, pepper and lemon juice. • Stir the prawns and dill into the cooled creamy sauce. • Take small balls of the dough and roll out into 6.5 cm/2½ in circles. Place a teaspoon of filling on one half of circle, dampen edges with water and fold in half. Press the two edges together, sealing with water. • Bring the water to the boil, add salt and oil, and cook the tortellini for about 6 minutes. Serve with grated cheese.

Pasta with Veal

A good midweek meal

Preparation time: 1¼ hours
Baking time: 10 minutes
Serves 4

250 g/9 oz/2¼ cups plain strong white flour
2 eggs
Pinch salt
350 g/12 oz stewing veal
100 g/4 oz lean streaky bacon
1 large onion
2 tomatoes
2 green peppers
1 tbsp pork dripping
1 tsp paprika
125 ml/4 fl oz/½ cup beef stock
3 litres/6 pt/12 cups water
1½ tsp salt (for water)
50 g/2 oz butter
100 g/4 oz/1 cup grated cheese

Using the flour, eggs, salt and as little water as needed, make a smooth firm dough and leave to rest, covered, for 30 minutes. • Mince the meat. Dice the bacon, peel the onion and chop finely. Peel and chop the tomatoes. Clean the green peppers and shred. • Fry the bacon in the pork dripping, and add the onion. Fry for 5 minutes together. Brown the meat, seasoning with salt and paprika. Stir in the tomatoes and strips of pepper. Pour the stock over and cook for 15 minutes. • Roll out the dough, but not too thinly, and cut into 4 cm/1½ in squares. Leave these to dry briefly, then cook for 4 minutes in salted water, and drain well. • Preheat the oven to 180°C/350°F/Gas Mark 4. Grease a baking dish with half the butter. • Stir the pasta into the veal mixture with 50 g/2 oz/½ cup cheese and turn into the baking dish and dot with dabs of butter. Bake for 10 min-

utes in the oven, and serve with the remaining grated cheese.

Ham Fleckerl

A Viennese speciality

Preparation time: 1½ hours
Baking time: 30 minutes
Serves 4

250 g/9 oz/2¼ cups plain strong white flour
5 eggs
2 pinches salt
175 g/6 oz cooked lean ham
100 g/4 oz softened butter
Pinch white pepper
Pinch grated nutmeg
125 g/4 oz soured cream
3 litres/6 pt/12 cups water
1½ tsp salt (for water)
4 tbsp white breadcrumbs
3 tbsp grated cheese

Make a firm dough from the flour, 2 eggs, 1 pinch salt and some water, and leave, covered, for 30 minutes. • Dice the ham. Separate the remaining eggs. Mix 50 g/2 oz butter with the egg yolks, and blend in the rest of the salt, pepper, nutmeg and soured cream. • Roll out the dough, but not too thinly, leave to dry, and cut into 4 cm/1½ in "fleckerl" (squares). Cook in boiling salted water for 4 minutes, and then add to the egg mixture with the ham. • Whisk the egg whites until stiff, and fold into the egg mixture carefully. • Preheat the oven to 200°C/400°F/Gas Mark 6. Grease baking dish well with butter, and sprinkle base with 2 tbsp of breadcrumbs. Add mixture, smoothing the top with a spoon, and sprinkle with the remaining crumbs and cheese. Drizzle with the melted butter and bake for 20 minutes.

Macaroni and Ham Pudding

Inexpensive

Preparation time: 30 minutes
Cooking time: 1½ hours
Serves 4

4 litres/8 pt water
2 tsp salt
2 tbsp oil
400 g/14 oz long macaroni
200 g/7 oz thinly sliced smoked ham
1 bunch chives
1 large onion, chopped
200 ml/7 fl oz/¾ cup & 2 tbsp double cream
4 eggs
Pinch salt and white pepper

Bring water and salt to the boil. Add 1 tsp oil and macaroni and cook for about 10 minutes until 'al dente'. • Chop smoked ham into small squares. Chop the chives finely. Heat the remaining oil and fry the onion gently, until softened. • Beat the cream and the eggs and stir in the onion. Add the salt, pepper, chives and ham. • Drain the macaroni and rinse in a colander under cold water. Dry the macaroni by spreading it on tea towels in a warm airy kitchen. • Butter a 1.1 litre/2 pt pudding basin and line with the cold macaroni. Then build up layers of macaroni and the ham and egg mixture in the centre, finishing with a layer of macaroni. • Cover with a pudding cloth or foil. Place in a saucepan three quarters of the way up the pudding basin. • The pudding should be cooked for approximately 1½ hours on a low heat. • Check the saucepan from time to time to make sure that the water does not boil away. • Serve the pudding turned out onto a hot dish. • Serve with a tomato sauce and fresh herbs.

Lasagne Al Forno

An Italian classic

Preparation time: 2 hours
Cooking time: 30–40 minutes
Serves 4–6

For the meat sauce:

2 onions

2 carrots

2 sticks celery

100 g/4 oz lean streaky bacon

350 g/12 oz minced beef

50 g/2 oz butter

125 ml/4 fl oz/½ cup red wine

350 ml/12 fl oz/1½ cups hot beef stock

1 tbsp tomato purée (paste)

Pinch each salt and freshly ground black pepper

125 ml/4 fl oz/½ cup hot milk

For the Bechamel sauce:

50 g/2 oz butter

50 g/2 oz/½ cup plain flour

600 ml/1 pt/2½ cups milk

Pinch each salt and white pepper

Pinch ground nutmeg

For the lasagne sheets:

3 eggs

Pinch salt

275 g/10 oz/2½ cups plain strong white flour

4 litres/8 pt water

1 tsp each oil and salt (for the water)

200 g/7 oz Mozzarella cheese

4 tbsp grated Parmesan cheese

2 tbsp butter

Peel onions, trim carrots, wash and dry celery. Chop vegetables finely. • Melt the butter, add the vegetables, bacon and meat and cook until lightly browned. Add salt and pepper to taste. • Add the wine and 125 ml/4 fl oz/½ cup beef stock and simmer until liquid is absorbed. Mix in the remaining stock with the tomato purée. Add salt and pepper to taste. Stir in the milk and simmer over a very low heat for approximately 1½ hours, stirring occasionally. • Meanwhile make the Bechamel sauce. Melt butter in a saucepan, add the flour and cook for 1 minute, without browning. Gradually add the milk, stirring constantly. Bring to the boil and simmer for 2 minutes. Season with salt, pepper and nutmeg. • Make pasta. Put eggs and salt into centre of flour in a bowl and mix by hand to a stiff, firm dough. Add cold water as needed. Cover the dough with a wet paper towel and leave for 1 hour. • Divide dough into portions and roll out each piece as thinly as possible on a lightly floured board or table top. • Cut into pieces, about 15 × 7 cm/6 × 2¾ in wide, with a sharp knife. • Bring water, salt and oil to the boil. Slowly drop in the lasagne and boil for about 4 minutes. • Drain on tea towels. • Dice the Mozzarella. • Preheat the oven to 180°C/350°F/Gas Mark 4. • Butter a large ovenproof dish and spoon in enough meat sauce to cover the base. Arrange a layer of lasagne sheets on top of the sauce followed by a layer of Bechamel sauce. • Mix some Mozzarella and Parmesan cheese between the layers. Repeat the layers until all the sauce, lasagne and Bechamel are used, finishing with a layer of Bechamel. Sprinkle with remaining cheese and a few dabs of butter. • Bake in preheated oven for 30–40 minutes until golden brown.

Lasagne with Spinach

Another Italian speciality

Preparation time: 45 minutes
Cooking time: 30 minutes
Serves 4

700 g/1½ lb spinach
600 ml/1 pt/2½ cups water
½ tsp salt
50 g/2 oz butter
50 g/2 oz/½ cup plain flour
250 ml/8 fl oz/1 cup milk
Pinch each ground nutmeg and white pepper
100 g/4 oz ricotta
100 g/4 oz Parmesan
2 large tomatoes
250 g/9 oz lasagne
2.5 litres/5 pt/10 cups water
1 tsp each salt and olive oil (for the water)
½ tsp dried oregano

Preheat the oven to 200°C/400°F/Gas Mark 6. Wash the spinach thoroughly and cook in boiling water for 2 minutes. Drain well and keep the liquid. • Melt the butter and stir in the flour, milk and spinach liquid until light yellow. Add the nutmeg and pepper to the Bechamel sauce to taste. Mix in the ricotta. Grate the Parmesan. Wash, dry and slice the tomatoes. • Cook the lasagne until 'al dente', and drain thoroughly. • Line the base of a large buttered ovenproof dish with lasagne. Spoon over some spinach, top with tomatoes and sprinkle with oregano and Parmesan. • Pour on the Bechamel sauce. • Repeat the layers finishing with lasagne and Bechamel sauce and bake on the middle shelf for 30 minutes.

Lasagne with Savoy Cabbage

Easy to prepare

Preparation time: 1 hour
Cooking time: 40 minutes
Serves 4

500 g/18 oz Savoy cabbage
Salt
1 onion
1 garlic clove
2 tbsp oil
400 g/14 oz minced beef
½ tsp dried thyme
Pinch black pepper
250 g/9 oz lasagne
2.5 litres/5 pt/10 cups water
50 g/2 oz butter
3 tbsp plain flour
250 ml/8 fl oz/1 cup milk
100 g/4 oz/¾ cup cream cheese with herbs
4 large tomatoes
100 g/4 oz Mozzarella cheese, chopped

Preheat oven to 200°C/400°F Gas Mark 6. Chop the cabbage and cook in a saucepan of boiling salted water for 2 minutes. Drain and keep 250 ml/8 fl oz/1 cup of the liquid. • Peel onion and garlic, chop finely and fry in oil with the beef, thyme, salt and pepper for 15 minutes. • Boil lasagne in salted water for approximately 5 minutes. Drain well. • Melt the butter in a saucepan, add flour, cooking liquid and milk and bring to a boil. Stir in the cream cheese. • Mix the cabbage, sliced tomatoes and Mozzarella with half the sauce. • Transfer a little bit of sauce to a buttered ovenproof dish and repeat layers of lasagne, cabbage, minced beef, tomatoes and cheese. • Spoon the remaining sauce over. • Bake in oven for 40 minutes.

Wholewheat Lasagne

Whole and hearty

Preparation time: 2 hours
Cooking time: 30 minutes
Serves 4

250 g/9 oz/2¼ cups wholewheat flour
2 tbsp sunflower oil
1½ tsp sea salt
2 eggs
500 g/18 oz leeks
100 g/4 oz mushrooms
4 tbsp olive oil
400 g/14 oz minced beef
½ tsp black pepper
250 ml/8 fl oz/1 cup water
125 ml/4 fl oz/½ cup double cream
2 tsp paprika
4 tbsp chopped fresh parsley
200 g/7 oz Emmental cheese
50 g/2 oz Parmesan cheese
500 g/18 oz large tomatoes
50 g/2 oz butter

Mix together flour, oil, salt and eggs in a bowl and make a firm dough. • Trim, clean and slice the leeks finely. Wash mushrooms, slice into thin slices and fry leeks and mushrooms in hot olive oil for 5 minutes until brown. • Stir in minced beef, add salt, pepper and water and simmer over a low heat for approximately 5 minutes. • Pour in the cream, paprika and parsley and allow the sauce to thicken. Grate the cheese. Slice tomatoes. Roll out the dough as thinly as possible and cut into rectangles. Boil the lasagne in salted water for 4 minutes. Drain well. • Make layers of lasagne, meat sauce, cheese and tomatoes in a well-buttered ovenproof dish. Finish layers with lasagne, tomatoes and finally cheese, dot with butter and bake in a preheated oven at 200°C/400°F/Gas Mark 6 for 30 minutes until golden brown.

Jollini Pie

Easy to prepare

Preparation time: 20 minutes
Cooking time: 30 minutes
Serves 4

3 litres/6 pt/12 cups water
Salt
1 tsp oil
275 g/10 oz jollini (pasta spirals)
275 g/10 oz/2 cups frozen peas
175 g/6 oz courgettes (zucchini)
100 g/4 oz salami
4 tbsp snipped chives
2 eggs
125 ml/4 fl oz/½ cup soured cream
50 g/2 oz/½ cup grated cheddar
40 g/1½ oz butter

Place the pasta spirals in boiling, salted water with the oil and cook for approximately 8 minutes until 'al dente'. • Boil the peas in 4 tbsp of salted water for 5 minutes. • Trim, clean and dice the courgettes. • Preheat the oven to 200°C/400°F/Gas Mark 6.
• Drain the pasta. Cut the salami into small pieces. • Place the pasta, salami, peas, courgettes (zucchini) and chives in a well-buttered ovenproof dish. • In a bowl, beat the eggs well, then beat in the soured cream and a pinch of salt and pour over the pasta mixture. • Sprinkle the cheese over the top and dot with butter. • Bake on middle shelf for 30 minutes until golden brown.

Pasta Casserole

Inexpensive and easy

Preparation time: 30 minutes
Cooking time: 40 minutes
Serves 4

1 litre/2 pt/4 cups water
350 g/12 oz macaroni or penne
1 small onion
275 g/10 oz cooked ham
2 eggs
Pinch ground nutmeg
1½ tsp salt
600 ml/1 pt/2½ cups milk
½ tsp cornflour
50 g/2 oz/½ cup grated Emmental cheese
4 tbsp breadcrumbs
40 g/1½ oz butter

Preheat oven to 200°C/400°F/Gas Mark 6. Bring a large saucepan of salted water to the boil. • Add the pasta and peeled onion and cook until 'al dente'. Dice the ham. • Beat the eggs well, then beat in the nutmeg, salt, milk and cornflour. • Drain the pasta thoroughly, discard onion and mix with the diced ham in a well buttered ovenproof dish.
• Pour the egg mixture over. • Sprinkle the Emmental cheese and breadcrumbs over the top. Dot with butter. • Place on the middle shelf of oven and bake for approximately 30 minutes until golden brown.

Spaghetti Gratin with Salami

A family favourite

Preparation time: 20 minutes
Cooking time: 30 minutes
Serves 4

400 g/14 oz spaghetti
4 litres/8 pt water
2 tsp salt
400 g/14 oz can peeled tomatoes
1 tsp dried oregano
Pinch white pepper
2 onions
1 garlic clove
50 g/2 oz salami, cut into thin slices
200 ml/7 fl oz/¾ cup soured cream
1 tbsp olive oil
3 tbsp grated Parmesan cheese
2 tbsp breadcrumbs

Preheat the oven to 200°C/400°F/Gas Mark 6. • Cook the spaghetti in boiling, salted water for 8 minutes until 'al dente.' • Mash the tomatoes. Add oregano, salt and pepper to taste. • Peel onions and cut into rings. Peel garlic clove and chop finely. • Place the spaghetti and tomato purée in an ovenproof dish greased with olive oil. • Put the onion rings on top. Add the salami slices. • Mix the soured cream, garlic and oil and pour over the salami slices. • Sprinkle the cheese and breadcrumbs over the top. • Bake on middle shelf of hot oven for approximately 30 minutes until lightly golden. • Serve with a mixed salad and fresh herbs.

Pasta with Cheese

Easy; a great supper dish

Preparation time: 25 minutes
Cooking time: 30 minutes
Serves 4

4 litres/8 pts water
400 g/14 oz pasta (tagliatelle or pasta twists)
2 tbsp salt
1 tbsp oil
400 g/14 oz Gruyère or Emmental cheese
125 ml/4 fl oz/½ cup double cream
Pinch salt and ground nutmeg
1 egg yolk
2 tbsp butter
2 tbsp chopped fresh parsley

Drop the pasta into boiling, salted water with the oil and cook until 'al dente.' Drain well. • Grate the cheese. • Whisk the cream, salt, nutmeg, and egg yolk until thick. • Place half the pasta in a buttered ovenproof dish. Add the cheese and finish with the remaining pasta. Pour cream over the top and dot with butter. • Bake at 200°C/400°F/Gas Mark 6 for 20–25 minutes until golden. • Sprinkle with parsley before serving. • Serve with a fresh green salad.

Noodle Nests with Bean Sprouts

Very tasty

Preparation time: 30 minutes
Serves 4

200 g/7 oz wholewheat vermicelli
2 litres/4 pt/ 8 cups water
1 tsp salt
150 g/5 oz bean sprouts
6 eggs
Pinch curry powder
2 tbsp soy sauce
8 small lettuce leaves
50 g/2 oz butter
175 g/6 oz Emmental cheese in 4 slices
50 g/2 oz thinly sliced ham
8 small basil leaves

Place the pasta in boiling, salted water and cook for 4 minutes. • Put in a colander, hold under cold running water. Drain well. • Rinse the bean sprouts under running water and drain. • Hardboil 4 eggs for 10 minutes and cut into halves. • Mix pasta, bean sprouts, curry and soy sauce and the remaining eggs together. • Wash and dry lettuce leaves and place on 4 serving plates. • Melt butter in a large frying pan and add the pasta, forming it into 8 small "nests." • Make a small hollow in the centre of the nests and place the ham and cheese slices inside. Place the egg halves on top and fold the ham and cheese slices over. • Fry the pasta for approximately 10 minutes over a low heat. • Serve on top of lettuce leaves, garnished with basil.

Pasta with Mushrooms

Great midweek meal

Preparation time: 30 minutes
Cooking time: 40 minutes
Serves 4

275 g/10 oz pasta twists
2.5 litres/5 pt/10 cups water
1 tsp salt
225 g/8 oz broccoli
225 g/8 oz button mushrooms
1 garlic clove
2 tbsp oil
2 eggs
600 ml/1 pt/2½ cups milk
Pinch salt, paprika and ground nutmeg
100 g/4 oz/1 cup grated Parmesan cheese
1 tbsp almond flakes
1 tbsp sesame seeds
1 tbsp melted butter

Preheat the oven to 230°C/450°F/Gas Mark 8. • Cook the pasta in boiling, salted water until 'al dente'. • Trim, clean and slice the broccoli and mushrooms. Peel the garlic and fry in half the oil. Add the broccoli and sauté for 3 minutes. • Heat the remaining oil and fry the mushrooms until golden brown. Drain the pasta. • Place the pasta spirals, broccoli and mushrooms in a well-buttered ovenproof dish. • Separate egg whites and egg yolks. • In a bowl, beat the egg yolks well, then beat in the milk, salt, paprika, nutmeg and the Parmesan cheese. • Whisk the egg whites until firm peaks form, but not until totally stiff. Mix with the egg yolks and pour over the top. • Sprinkle the almond flakes and sesame seeds on top and pour the butter over. • Bake for 40 minutes.

Macaroni Pie with Aubergines (Eggplants)

Popular supper dish

Preparation time: 1 hour
Cooking time: 30 minutes
Serves 4

3 small aubergines (eggplants)
1 tbsp salt
400 g/14 oz macaroni
4 litres/8 pt water
1 bunch spring onions
2 carrots
150 g/5 oz celery
1 sprig thyme
125 ml/4 fl oz/½ cup olive oil
400 g/14 oz canned peeled tomatoes
100 g/4 oz/1 cup grated cheddar cheese
150 g/5 oz Mozzarella cheese

Preheat the oven to 220°C/425°F/Gas Mark 7. • Cut the aubergines (eggplants) into 1 cm/⅓ in slices. Lightly salt and leave for 20 minutes. • Break the pasta in half and cook in boiling, salted water until 'al dente'. • Trim, clean and finely chop the onions, carrots and celery. • Fry the chopped thyme leaves and the vegetables in 2 tbsp of oil. Add the tomatoes and simmer for approximately 10 minutes. • Rinse and dry the aubergines (eggplants) and fry in the remaining oil until brown. • Place half the macaroni in a buttered ovenproof dish. Spread 2 tbsp of grated cheddar on top. Pour the tomato sauce over. Add the aubergines (eggplants) and remaining pasta in layers on top. • Finish with the Mozzarella cheese slices and bake for 30 minutes.

Wholewheat Shells with Fennel

Healthy and inexpensive

Preparation time: 25 minutes
Cooking time: 30 minutes
Serves 4

500 g/18 oz fennel
275 g/10 oz wholewheat pasta shells or rigatoni
2.5 litres/5 pt/10 cups water
1 tsp salt (for the water)
4 eggs
250 ml/8 fl oz/1 cup single (light) cream
2 tbsp wholemeal flour
6 tbsp tomato purée (paste)
1 tsp dried mixed herbs
Pinch white pepper
2 tsp sea salt
4 tbsp chopped fresh parsley
200 g/7 oz Gouda cheese, cut in slices
50 g/2 oz butter

Preheat the oven to 180°C/350°F/Gas Mark 4. • Wash the fennel in cold water, dry thoroughly and cut into thin strips. • Save feathery leaves from the fennel for the garnish. • Cook the pasta and fennel together in boiling, salted water for approximately 8 minutes until tender. • Drain well. • In a bowl, beat the eggs well, then beat in the cream, flour, tomato purée (paste), herbs, seasoning and 2 tsp chopped parsley. • Place the pasta and fennel in an ovenproof dish. • Pour the egg mixture over and bake for 20 minutes. • Place the cheese slices and dabs of butter on top and bake for another 10 minutes. • Sprinkle with remaining parsley and fennel leaves before serving.

Tagliatelle Pie with Tomatoes

Easy and popular

Preparation time: 30 minutes
Cooking time: 20–30 minutes
Serves 4

225 g/10 oz tagliatelle
2.5 litres/5 pt/10 cups water
1 tsp salt (for the water)
1 bulb of fennel
3 large tomatoes
1 bunch mixed herbs, e.g. chervil, sage, dill
40 g/1½ oz butter
125 ml/4 fl oz/½ cup single (light) cream
100 g/4 oz cooked ham
2 eggs
150 ml/5 fl oz/⅔ cup soured cream
125 ml/4 fl oz/½ cup milk
Pinch salt and freshly milled white pepper
2 tbsp breadcrumbs

Preheat the oven to 200°C/400°F/Gas Mark 6. • Cook the pasta in boiling, salted water until tender. • Wash the fennel in cold water, dry thoroughly and cut into thin strips. • Trim feathery leaves from the fennel and save for garnish. • Slice the tomatoes and reserve a few slices for garnish. Wash and dry the herbs. • Fry the fennel in 15 g/½ oz butter. Add the cream, herbs and diced ham. • Butter an ovenproof dish. Place the pasta, fennel and tomatoes in layers in the dish. • Beat the eggs well, then beat in the soured cream, milk and salt and pepper to taste, and pour over the top. • Sprinkle with breadcrumbs and a few dabs of butter and bake for approximately 20–30 minutes. Garnish with tomatoes slices and fennel leaves.

Pasta Soufflé with Smoked Salmon

An exquisite dish

Preparation time: 30 minutes
Cooking time: 30 minutes
Serves 4

250 g/9 oz small pasta shapes (e.g. pasta bows, elbow macaroni, etc.)
2.5 litres/5 pt/10 cups water
1 tsp salt
6 eggs
250 ml/8 fl oz/1 cup single (light) cream
125 ml/4 fl oz/½ cup milk
Pinch of salt and white pepper
150 g/6 oz/1½ cups grated Gruyère cheese
½ tsp paprika
150 g/6 oz smoked salmon
1 bunch chives

Preheat the oven to 180°C/350°F/Gas Mark 4. • Cook the pasta in boiling, salted water for approximately 8 minutes until 'al dente'. • Hold under cold running water and drain well. • Separate the egg yolks from the egg whites. • Beat the egg yolks, then beat in the cream, milk, salt and pepper to taste. • Whisk egg whites until firm peaks form. Take half the cheese and paprika and beat into the stiff egg white. Fold into egg yolk mixture. • Dice the salmon. Wash, dry and finely chop the chives. • Mix the pasta, salmon and chives together. Add salt and pepper to taste. • Butter four small ovenproof dishes. Place the pasta into the dishes and pour the egg mixture over. • Sprinkle with the remaining cheese. • Place the dishes on the middle shelf of the oven and bake for approximately 30 minutes until golden brown. • Serve with white wine sauce or tomato salad with basil.

Macaroni Pie

A midweek surprise

Preparation time: 50 minutes
Cooking time: 40 minutes
Serves 4

225 g/8 oz/2 cups wholewheat flour

½ tsp salt

100 g/4 oz butter

1 egg, beaten

1 kg/2¼ lb tomatoes

3 garlic cloves

4 tbsp olive oil

2 tsp fresh chopped marjoram and basil

Pinch black pepper

200 g/7 oz wholewheat macaroni

2 litres/4 pt/8 cups water

1 tsp salt (for the water)

75 g/3 oz/⅔ cup black olives

150 g/5 oz cheddar cheese

1 tbsp butter

Preheat the oven to 180°C/350°F/Gas Mark 4. Mix together flour and salt. Rub in butter and then form into a dough with the beaten egg and a little water, if necessary. Cover and put in a cool place. • Skin and dice the tomatoes. Peel the garlic clove and fry in oil until transparent. • Add the herbs, tomatoes and pepper. Cook for 15 minutes, until liquid evaporates. • Break the macaroni into pieces and boil in salted water until tender and drain. • Stone olives and cut into small pieces. • Grate the cheese. Mix the pasta, olives, cheese and the tomato mixture. • Butter an ovenproof dish. Roll out the dough thinly and use to line the dish. Roll out remainder for top. • Place the pasta in the dish, top with pastry cover and press firmly around the edges. Pierce a few holes in the top. • Glaze with butter. • Bake for 40 minutes until golden brown.

Pasta Pizza

Easy

Preparation time: 40 minutes
Cooking time: 30 minutes
Serves 6

500 g/18 oz spaghetti

5 litres/10 pt water

2 tsp salt (for the water)

2 green peppers

200 g/7 oz salami, thinly sliced

500 g/18 oz tomatoes

8 eggs

350 ml/12 fl oz/1½ cups milk

1 tbsp cornflour

100 g/4 oz/1 cup grated Parmesan cheese

2 tbsp each Italian herbs, paprika and chopped basil

1 tsp salt

275 g/10 oz Emmental cheese

4 tbsp olive oil

2 tbsp chives

Preheat the oven to 180°C/350°F/Gas Mark 4. • Cook the pasta in boiling, salted water for 6 minutes. Clean and chop the green peppers. Add to the pasta and cook for another 2 minutes. Drain in a colander. • Butter two ovenproof dishes. • Put the pasta and green peppers in each of the dishes. • Place salami slices on top. • Wash and slice tomatoes and place on top of the salami. • Mix the eggs, milk, cornflour, Parmesan and herbs and pour over the top. • Grate the Emmental cheese and sprinkle on top. • Pour the oil over. • Bake the pizzas for approximately 30 minutes. • Sprinkle with chives before serving.

Macaroni Bake

Lengthy cooking time

Preparation time: 1 hour
Cooking time: 40–45 minutes
Serves 4

600 g/1¼ lb veal escalopes
4 tbsp oil
2 bay leaves
125 ml/4 fl oz/½ cup dry white wine
125 ml/4 fl oz/½ cup soured cream
5 eggs
Pinch salt and pepper
1 tsp dried tarragon
400 g/14 oz macaroni
4 litres/8 pt water
2 tsp salt
150 g/5 oz Emmental cheese
1 bunch parsley, chopped
1 onion
125 ml/4 fl oz/½ cup single (light) cream

Preheat the oven to 200°C/400°F/Gas Mark 6. • Dice the veal escalopes and fry in 2 tbsp oil. Add the bay leaves and the wine. Cover the meat and cook for 30 minutes. Leave to cool and then mince. Add soured cream and 1 egg to the minced meat. Add salt, pepper and tarragon to taste. • Cook the macaroni in boiling, salted water for 8 minutes. Drain well. Pour the remaining oil over. Grate the cheese. • Place half the macaroni in a buttered dish, add the minced meat and sprinkle the parsley on top. • Peel and chop the onion. Scatter over the meat with half the grated cheese and add the remaining macaroni. • Mix the remaining eggs with the cream. Add the salt and pepper to taste and pour over the macaroni. • Bake for 30 minutes. • Sprinkle remaining cheese on top and bake for another 10–15 minutes until golden brown and crispy.

Wholewheat Macaroni with Spinach

A simple, nutritious dish

Preparation time: 45 minutes
Cooking time: 35 minutes
Serves 4

250 g/9 oz wholewheat macaroni
2.5 litres/5 pt/10 cups water
1 tsp salt (for the water)
1 tsp oil
1.5 kg/3½ lb spinach
1 onion
2 garlic cloves
50 g/2 oz butter
50 g/2 oz/½ cup wholewheat flour
125 ml/4 fl oz/½ cup hot vegetable stock
250 ml/8 fl oz/1 cup single (light) cream
150 g/5 oz Gouda cheese
Pinch white pepper

Preheat the oven to 200°C/400°F/Gas Mark 6. • Cook the pasta in boiling, salted water with the oil until 'al dente'. Drain well. • Clean and wash the spinach and cook for 2 minutes until wilted. • Peel and chop the onion and garlic. Fry in butter until transparent. • Add the flour and fry until pale. Pour in the stock and cream and bring to the boil, stirring constantly. • Grate the cheese and stir into the sauce. Season with salt and pepper to taste. • Place half the macaroni in a buttered dish. Add the spinach and a third of the cheese sauce. • Place the remaining pasta and cheese sauce on top. • Bake for 35 minutes.

Russian Cobbler

A hearty meal in itself

Preparation time: 35 minutes
Cooking time: 40 minutes
Serves 4

250 g/9 oz tagliatelle
2.5 litres/5 pt/10 cups water
1 tsp salt
200 g/7 oz streaky bacon
2 onions
½ tsp dried marjoram
500 g/18 oz ricotta
2 eggs
100 ml/4 fl oz/½ cup single (light) cream
Pinch freshly milled white pepper and salt
75 g/3 oz butter
4 tbsp breadcrumbs
2 tbsp chopped parsley

Preheat the oven to 180°C/350°F/Gas Mark 4. • Cook the pasta in boiling, salted water until 'al dente'. Drain in a colander. • Cut the bacon into small pieces. Peel and chop the onions. Fry the bacon and onions until transparent. Stir in the pasta and marjoram. • In a bowl, beat together the ricotta, cream and eggs. Season with salt and pepper. • Place three-quarters of the pasta in an ovenproof dish. • Add the ricotta mixture and finish layering with the remaining pasta. • Sprinkle the butter and breadcrumbs on top of the pasta. • Bake on the middle shelf of the oven for 30 minutes. • Place dish under grill and cook until crispy. • Sprinkle with parsley before serving.

Turkish Pasta Pie

Inexpensive

Preparation time: 35 minutes
Cooking time: 30 minutes
Serves 4

3 litres/6 pt/12 cups water
1 tsp salt (for the water)
350 g/12 oz macaroni
50 g/2 oz butter
3 tbsp plain flour
600 ml/1 pt/2½ cups milk
3 eggs
Pinch white pepper
50 g/2 oz/½ cup chopped walnuts
50 g/2 oz/½ cup grated Cheddar

Preheat the oven to 200°C/400°F/Gas Mark 6. • Cook the macaroni in boiling, salted water until 'al dente'. Drain in a colander, hold under cold running water. • Melt the butter in a saucepan. Add the flour and heat, stirring until light yellow. Pour in the milk and stir constantly. Simmer for 10 minutes. Leave to cool. Beat the eggs well, then beat in the pepper. • Pour the sauce into a buttered ovenproof dish and place the pasta on top. • Sprinkle with walnuts. • Pour remaining sauce and cheese over. • Bake for 30 minutes until golden brown. • Serve with tomato salad and onion rings or black olives.

Macaroni Pie with Onions

Robust flavour

Preparation time: 1 hour
Cooking time: 30 minutes
Serves 4

250 g/9 oz macaroni
2.5 litres/5 pt/10 cups water
Salt
1 kg/2¼ lb large onions
1 garlic clove
3 tbsp oil
Pinch freshly ground black pepper
4 eggs
125 ml/4 fl oz/½ cup soured cream
100 g/4 oz/1 cup grated Emmental cheese
2 tsp paprika ·
2 tbsp chopped fresh parsley

Preheat the oven to 200°C/400°F/Gas Mark 6. • Drop the macaroni in boiling, salted water and cook for 10 minutes until tender. Drain in a colander. • Peel and chop the onions and garlic. • Heat the oil and fry onions and garlic until transparent. Season with salt and pepper to taste. • In a bowl, whisk the eggs, soured cream, grated cheese, paprika and parsley. • Place half the onions in a buttered ovenproof dish. Add the macaroni and put the remaining onions on top. • Pour the creamy cheese mixture over. • Place in the oven and bake for 30 minutes until golden brown.

Macaroni Pie with Minced Beef

A speciality from Greece

Preparation time: 1½ hours
Cooking time: 40 minutes
Serves 4

250 g/9 oz macaroni
2.5 litres/5 pt/10 cups water
Salt
75 g/3 oz butter
1 egg white
6 tbsp grated Parmesan cheese
1 large onion
500 g/1 lb 2 oz minced beef
Pinch each white pepper and cinnamon
4 large tomatoes
125 ml/4 fl oz/½ cup beef stock
125 ml/4 fl oz ½ cup dry white wine
2 tbsp chopped fresh parsley
2 tbsp plain flour
350 ml/12 fl oz/1½ cups milk
4 tbsp breadcrumbs

Preheat the oven to 200°C/400°F/Gas Mark 6. • Cook the macaroni in salted water for approximately 8 minutes until 'al dente'. Drain. • Melt 25 g/1 oz of the butter in a saucepan and fry macaroni for 2 minutes. • Whisk the egg white until firm peaks form, then fold in the macaroni and 2 tbsp Parmesan. • Place half of the macaroni in a well buttered ovenproof dish. • Peel and chop the onion and fry in 25 g/1 oz butter until transparent. • Add the minced beef, salt, pepper and cinnamon and fry until meat browns. Peel the tomatoes and add to meat with stock. Simmer for approximately 15 minutes. Pour in the wine and add the parsley. • Place some meat mixture on top of the macaroni and continue to layer with the remaining pasta. • Mix flour with 2 tbsp of water. Bring milk to the boil. Stir in the flour mixture and simmer for a few minutes. • Add salt and remaining grated cheese to taste. Pour the sauce over the pasta. • Sprinkle the breadcrumbs and remaining butter on top. • Bake the pie on the middle shelf for approximately 40 minutes. • Serve with a green salad.

Macaroni Casserole

A speciality from Greece

Preparation time: 1¼ hours
Cooking time: 45 minutes
Serves 4

| 3 onions |
| 2 large garlic cloves |
| 1 leek |
| 1 celery stalk |
| 1 carrot |
| 1 bunch parsley |
| 50 g/2 oz butter |
| 500 g/1 lb 2 oz minced lamb or veal |
| Salt and freshly ground black pepper |
| 125 ml/4 fl oz/½ cup dry red wine |
| 275 ml/8 fl oz/1 cup hot beef stock |
| 3 litres/6 pt/12 cups water |

| 350 g/12 oz macaroni |
| 500 g/18 oz tomatoes |
| 100 g/4 oz Parmesan cheese |

Peel and chop the onions and garlic. • Trim, wash, dry and dice the leek and celery. • Wash, peel and dice the carrot. • Wash, dry and chop the parsley. • Melt half the butter in a saucepan. Add the onions and fry until transparent. Stir in the garlic, leek, celery and carrot. • Add the minced meat and fry until brown. • Stir in the parsley, salt, pepper and red wine. Simmer in an uncovered saucepan until liquid evaporates. • Add the meat stock and simmer for another 30 minutes. • Cook the macaroni in boiling, salted water for approximately 8 minutes until 'al dente'. Drain well. • Cool an earthenware dish in cold water. • Peel and chop the tomatoes. • Place half the macaroni in the earthenware dish. Add the minced meat sauce. Put the remaining macaroni on top. Season with salt and pepper to taste and add the tomatoes. • Cover the earthenware dish and put into a cold oven. Set oven at 220°C/450°F/Gas Mark 8 and bake for 30 minutes. • Grate the cheese and sprinkle on top. Add a few dabs of butter and bake uncovered for an additional 15 minutes until golden brown and crispy. • Vegetarians can use courgettes instead of minced meat.

Neapolitan Macaroni Pie

A speciality from Italy

Preparation time: 1¼ hours
Cooking time: 20–30 minutes
Serves 4

2 aubergines (eggplants)
Salt
500 g/18 oz tomatoes
1 onion
1 carrot
1 celery stalk
½ bunch basil, chopped
6 tbsp olive oil
Pinch of black pepper
250 g/9 oz macaroni
2.5 litres/5 pt/10 cups water
1 tsp salt
100 g/4 oz/1 cup grated Parmesan cheese
200 g/7 oz Mozzarella cheese

Preheat the oven to 220°C/450°F/Gas Mark 8. • Wash, dry and slice aubergines (eggplants). Sprinkle with 2 tsp salt and leave for 30 minutes. • Peel and cut the tomatoes into pieces. • Peel the onion. Grate the carrot. • Trim, clean and chop the celery. • Heat half the oil and fry the onion, carrot and celery. • Add the tomatoes and basil, then season with salt and pepper to taste. • Simmer until thickened. • Rinse and dry the aubergines (eggplants). Heat the remaining oil and fry the aubergines (eggplants) until brown. • Break the macaroni into pieces and drop into boiling, salted water. Cook until tender. • Place half the macaroni with half the sauce in a well buttered oven-proof dish. Add the grated Parmesan. • Cover with half the aubergines (eggplants). Place half the Mozzarella on top. • Finish with the remaining pasta, aubergines (eggplants) and Mozzarella slices. • Pour the remaining sauce over and bake for 20–30 minutes.

Great Pasta Salads

Rigatoni Salad with Cheese, Tomatoes and Cress

Easy and colourful

Preparation time: 30 minutes
Cooling time: 1–2 hours
Serves 4

225 g/8 oz elbow macaroni
2 litres/4 pt/8 cups water
3 tbsp vinegar
1 tsp salt (for the water)
Pinch of white pepper
2 eggs
2 bunches radishes
1 bunch cress
½ bunch parsley
4 tomatoes
100 g/4 oz Emmental cheese
200 ml/7 fl oz/¾ cup soured cream

Drop the rigatoni into boiling, salted water and cook for approximately 8 minutes until 'al dente'. Rinse and drain. Season with vinegar, salt and pepper to taste. • Boil the eggs for 10 minutes. Hold under cold running water, peel and slice. • Trim, wash and slice the radishes. • Hold the cress and parsley under running water, drain and chop finely. • Wash, seed and slice the tomatoes into wedges. Dice the cheese. • In a bowl, mix together the radishes, herbs, cheese, soured cream and pasta. Add the tomatoes and eggs. • Put the salad in the refrigerator for 1–2 hours. • Leave at room temperature for 10 minutes before serving.

Multi-coloured Pasta Salad

Easy to prepare

Preparation time: 40 minutes
Serves 4

275 g/10 oz multi-coloured pasta
2.5 litres/5 pt/10 cups water
1 tsp salt
250 g/9 oz/1¼ cups natural yogurt
3 tbsp lemon juice
2 tsp sugar
Pinch salt
125 ml/4 fl oz/½ cup double cream
200 g/7 oz Emmental cheese
75 g/3 oz/¾ cup walnuts
250 g/9 oz black grapes
1 red apple
1 pear
½ curly endive

Drop the pasta into boiling, salted water for 6-8 minutes and cook until 'al dente'. Rinse and drain. • In a bowl, mix together the yogurt, lemon juice, sugar and salt. • Beat the cream until stiff and stir into the yogurt mixture. • Cut cheese into thin strips. Chop the walnuts. • Wash and stone the grapes and halve. Thinly slice the apple and pear and remove cores. • In a bowl, mix together the nuts, cheese, pasta, fruit and yogurt mixture. • Trim and wash the endive and dry thoroughly. • Separate the endive into leaves, tear into pieces and arrange on 4 serving dishes. Serve pasta salad on top.

Pasta and Parma Ham Salad

An Italian favourite

Preparation time: 30 minutes
Serves 4

400 g/14 oz spaghetti or macaroni
4 litres/8 pt water
2 tsp salt
175 g/6 oz Parma ham
10 black olives
150 g/5 oz Gorgonzola cheese
1 bunch basil
3–4 tbsp vinegar
Pinch each sugar and white pepper
4 tbsp olive oil
50 g/2 oz/⅓ cup pistachios

Drop the pasta into boiling, salted water and cook for 8 minutes. Rinse and drain. Leave to cool. • Cut the ham into thin strips. Stone the olives and halve them. Crumble cheese into pieces. Trim, wash and cut the basil into thin strips. • In a bowl, mix together the vinegar, pinch of salt, sugar, pepper and oil. • Chop the pistachios. Mix the pasta with the cheese, ham, olives and basil. • Pour the dressing over. Toss well and leave for 30 minutes. • Sprinkle with the pistachios.

Variation: Instead of Gorgonzola cheese use melon.

Roman Pasta Salad

A classic

Preparation time: 1 hour
Serves 4

400 g/14 oz macaroni
4 litres/8 pt water
1 tsp salt
2 carrots
225 g/8 oz/2 cups green beans
225 g/8 oz/2 cups frozen peas
3 tomatoes
100 g/4 oz Italian salami, thinly sliced
2 tbsp each green and black olives
6 anchovy fillets
2 tbsp capers
3 tbsp vinegar
4 tbsp olive oil
Pinch each salt, black pepper and sugar
3 tbsp snipped chives

Put the pasta into boiling, salted water and cook until 'al dente'. • Peel, wash and cut the carrots into slices. • Wash, trim and cut the green beans into pieces. Boil carrots in salted water for 12 minutes. • Boil the beans for 5 minutes and the peas for 2 minutes. • Wash and dry the tomatoes. Cut into eighths. • Cut the salami into thin slices. • Stone the green and black olives and halve them. • Chop the anchovies and mix with the capers, vinegar, oil and spices. • Drain the pasta and mix with the vegetables, tomatoes, salami, olives and dressing. Sprinkle with chives and leave covered for approximately 1 hour before serving.

Amsterdam Pasta Salad

Economical and easy

Preparation time: 40 minutes
Serves 4

275 g/10 oz pasta (macaroni or pasta spirals)	
2.5 litres/5 pt/10 cups water	
1 tsp salt (for the water)	
4 hard-boiled eggs	
6 small tomatoes	
1 small cucumber	
1 red pepper	
200 g/7 oz corned beef	
Pinch each salt and white pepper	
Pinch sugar and garlic powder	
2 tbsp vinegar	
3 tbsp oil	
½ bunch chopped parsley	

Drop pasta into boiling, salted water and cook until 'al dente'. Rinse and drain. • Peel eggs and cut into quarters. • Wash, dry and slice tomatoes and cucumber. • Halve the pepper, remove the core and seeds. Wash, dry and shred finely. • Slice the corned beef. • In a bowl, mix together the pasta, vegetables, corned beef and eggs. Mix together the salt, pepper, sugar, garlic powder, vinegar and oil. Stir into salad. • Cover and leave for 30 minutes at room temperature. • Wash and chop the parsley and sprinkle on top before serving.

Danish Pasta Salad

Economical and easy

Preparation time: 30 minutes
Cooling time: 1 hour
Serves 4

2.5 litres/5 pt/10 cups water	
1 tsp salt (for the water)	
250 g/9 oz pasta bows	
275 g/10 oz/2 cups frozen peas and carrots	
Pinch each salt and freshly ground black pepper	
2 slices pineapple	
1 large gherkin	
225 g/8 oz cooked lean ham	
200 ml/7 fl oz/¾–1 cup mayonnaise	
3 tbsp lemon juice	
2 tbsp pineapple juice	
½ tsp curry powder	

Drop the pasta into boiling, salted water and cook until tender. • Rinse and drain well. • Boil the peas and carrots in 4 tbsp of water. Add salt and pepper and simmer for an additional 4 minutes. • Leave to cool. • Remove the rind from the pineapple and cut into small pieces. • Dice the ham and gherkin. • In a bowl, mix together the mayonnaise, lemon and pineapple juice. Season with salt and pepper and curry powder to taste. • Pour over the pasta. Add vegetables, gherkin, tomatoes, pineapple and ham and mix well together. • Cover and leave for 1 hour in a cool place.

Pasta Salad with Chicken

A main meal salad

Preparation time: 45 minutes
Serves 4

½ roasted chicken
200 g/7 oz macaroni
2 litres/4 pt/8 cups water
1 tsp salt (for the water)
150 g/5 oz Gouda cheese
1 small endive
225 g/8 oz black grapes
150 g/5 oz/⅔ cup full fat yogurt
150 ml/5 fl oz/⅔ cup soured cream
1 bunch fresh mixed herbs (e.g., basil, chives, thyme)
Pinch each salt, white pepper and paprika
Juice of ½ lemon

Skin and bone the chicken. Cut flesh into small pieces. • Drop the pasta into boiling salted water and cook until tender. Rinse and drain. • Dice the cheese. Wash and drain the endive. Tear into pieces. Wash and stone the grapes. Cut into halves. • In a bowl, mix together the meat, pasta, cheese, endive and grapes. • Mix the yogurt and soured cream. • Wash, dry and chop the herbs and stir into the yogurt mixture. Add seasoning and lemon juice and stir well. • Pour the dressing over the salad. Mix well. Cover and leave for 45 minutes.

Variation: Instead of grapes use pineapple or chopped walnuts.

Indian Pasta Salad

An exotic speciality

Preparation time: 1 hour
Serves 4

4 chicken breasts
1 tsp coriander
2 tsp curry powder
Pinch white pepper and salt
6 tbsp oil
4 tbsp marsala wine
100 g/4 oz/¾ cup blanched almonds
2 bananas
1 tbsp lemon juice
2 tbsp raisins
2 litres/5 pt/10 cups water
1 tsp salt (for the water)
200 g/7 oz tagliatelle
4 tbsp light soy sauce

Place the chicken breasts in a large bowl and coat with ½ tsp coriander, curry powder, salt and pepper. • Heat half the oil in a saucepan. Add the chicken and brown all sides. Pour the marsala wine over and simmer over a low heat for 20 minutes. Leave to cool, reserving the stock. • Fry almonds in a saucepan until golden brown. • Peel and slice the bananas and sprinkle with lemon juice. • Wash and dry the raisins. • Dice the chicken and cut into pieces. Cook tagliatelle for 8–10 minutes in boiling, salted water. Drain and refresh in cold water. • In a bowl, mix together the remaining coriander and curry powder, soy sauce, salt and oil. Add the chicken, stock, bananas, almonds and raisins and toss well. • Mix with the pasta. Leave in a cool place for 2 hours. Season to taste before serving.

Arabian Pasta Salad

Economical and unusual

Preparation time: 20 minutes
Serves 4

400 g/14 oz rigatoni
4 litres/8 pt water
1 tsp salt (for the water)
1 cucumber
100 g/4 oz Feta cheese
½ bunch dill
½ lemon
1 tbsp apple juice
100 g/4 oz/½ cup set yogurt
1 tbsp mayonnaise
5 mint leaves
1 jar pickled pumpkin
2 tbsp sesame seeds

Put the pasta into boiling, salted water and cook until 'al dente'. • Peel and dice the cucumber. • Crumble the Feta cheese into pieces. • Wash, dry and chop the dill and mix with the lemon juice, apple juice, yogurt and mayonnaise. • Wash, dry and chop the mint leaves. • In a bowl, mix together the pasta, cucumber, pumpkin, Feta cheese and mint. • Pour lemon juice mixture over, toss well and leave for 30 minutes. • Fry the sesame seeds in a saucepan until golden brown, stirring constantly. • Sprinkle on top of the salad before serving.

Pasta Salad with Tuna Fish

A great favourite

Preparation time: 30 minutes
Serves 4

250 g/9 oz pasta shells

2.5 litres/5 pt/10 cups water

1 tsp salt (for the water)

1 can tuna fish in oil

2 slices pineapple

1 cooking apple

2 tbsp lemon juice

1 small onion

Pinch salt and freshly milled white pepper

1 tbsp walnut oil

½ tsp curry powder

1 tbsp pineapple juice

1 tbsp mustard

100 g/4 oz/⅔ cup prawns

Put the pasta into boiling, salted water and cook for 10 minutes until 'al dente'. Drain the tuna fish, reserving the oil. • Dice the pineapple slices. • Peel, core and quarter the apple. Cut into thin slices and sprinkle with half the lemon juice. • Peel and chop the onion and place in serving bowl. • Add the remaining lemon juice, salt, pepper, oil, curry powder, pineapple juice, mustard and the tuna fish oil. Mix well. • Stir in the pasta. Flake the tuna fish and add to the salad together with the prawns, apple slices and pineapple pieces. Mix well.

Pasta and Smoked Trout Salad

Easy to prepare

Preparation time: 45 minutes
Serves 4

250 g/9 oz pasta spirals

2.5 litres/5 pt/10 cups water

1 tsp salt (for the water)

4 smoked fillets of trout

500 g/18 oz tomatoes

2 gherkins

1 onion

3 tbsp vinegar

½ tsp salt

Pinch white pepper and sugar

3 tbsp olive oil

1 tablespoon chopped fresh chives

1 tablespoon chopped fresh chervil

Put the pasta into boiling, salted water and cook for 8 minutes until 'al dente'. Cut the trout fillets into small portions. • Put tomatoes into boiling water for 10 seconds, then place immediately into a bowl of cold water. Drain and skin the tomatoes, remove the seeds and cut into wedges. • Dice the gherkins. Peel and chop the onion and place in a bowl. Add vinegar, salt, pepper, sugar and oil and then add the cold pasta. Add the trout pieces, tomatoes and gherkin pickles. Mix well. • Season to taste and sprinkle with chopped chives and chervil before serving.

Tagliatelle with Red Lentils

Healthy and easy

Preparation time: 45 minutes
Serves 4

50 g/2 oz/⅓ cup dried figs and apricots
150 g/5 oz/¾ cup red lentils
600 ml/1 pt/2½ cups water
1 small bay leaf
½ vegetable stock cube
200 g/7 oz wholewheat tagliatelle
2 litres/4 pt/8 cups water
1 tsp salt (for the water)
50 g/2 oz smoked ham
50 g/2 oz/⅓ cup dates
200 ml/7 fl oz/¾ cup soured cream
3 tbsp lemon juice
Pinch freshly milled white pepper
1 tbsp chopped parsley

Wash the figs and apricots; put in a bowl and pour boiling water over. Cover and leave for approximately 15 minutes. • Place the lentils in boiling water. Add the bay leaf and vegetable stock and simmer over a low heat for 10 minutes. • Put the pasta into boiling, salted water and cook for approximately 10 minutes until 'al dente'. Drain the pasta and lentils. • Cut the smoked ham into thin strips. • Drain the figs and apricots and cut into thin strips. Pit the dates and cut into pieces. • In a bowl, mix together the soured cream, 2 tbsp lemon juice and pepper. Add all the chopped and cooked ingredients and mix well. Add remaining lemon juice and pepper to taste. • Leave at room temperature for 15 minutes and sprinkle with parsley before serving.

Wholewheat Pasta Salad with Chicken

Healthy

Preparation time: 50 minutes
Serves 4

100 g/4 oz/⅔ cup chickpeas

1 litre/1¾ pt/4 cups vegetable stock

200 g/7 oz wholewheat pasta (spirals or rigatoni)

2 litres/4 pt/8 cups water

Salt

1 roasted chicken

2 ripe avocados

100 g/4 oz mushrooms

100 g/4 oz carrots

150 ml/5 fl oz/⅔ cup single (light) cream

1 tsp honey

3 tbsp lemon juice

Pinch white pepper

2 tbsp chopped fresh parsley

Soak the chickpeas overnight in cold water. Drain. • The next day, place the chickpeas in a large saucepan together with the vegetable stock and simmer on a low heat for 40 minutes. • Drop the pasta into boiling, salted water and cook for 8–10 minutes. Drain and rinse. • Skin and bone the chicken and cut the meat into pieces. Halve and stone the avocados and cut flesh into pieces. • Clean the mushrooms, remove the stalks and slice finely. • Peel and coarsely grate the carrots. • In a bowl mix together the cream, honey, salt, 2 tbsp lemon juice, pepper and parsley. • Stir in all the vegetables and meat. Mix well. • Leave the salad to stand for 15 minutes before serving. • Add remaining lemon juice, salt and pepper to taste.

Chickpea and Pasta Salad

Takes time

Soaking time: 12 hours
Preparation time: 30 minutes
Serves 4

100 g/4 oz/⅔ cup chickpeas

2 tsp vegetable stock

1 small bay leaf

150 g/5 oz/1 cup blanched almonds

200 g/7 oz pasta spirals

2 litres/4 pt/8 cups water

1 tsp salt (for the water)

400 g/14 oz canned mandarin orange segments

200 g/7 oz/1 cup cottage cheese

100 ml/4 fl oz/½ cup single (light) cream

2 pinches salt and curry powder

2 tbsp lemon juice

Soak the chickpeas overnight in 1 litre/1¾ pts of cold water. • Drain and rinse. Place in a saucepan with vegetable stock cube and bay leaf, bring to the boil and simmer for about 1 hour until just tender. Drain. • Roast the almonds in a dry pan. • Drop the pasta into boiling salted water and cook for 8 minutes. Rinse and drain. • Cut the almonds into thin pieces. • Drain the mandarin oranges. • In a bowl mix together the cottage cheese, cream, salt, curry powder and lemon juice. • Pour in all the remaining ingredients and mix well.

Spaghetti Salad with Chicken

Healthy and easy

Preparation time: 40 minutes
Serves 4

| 2.5 litres/5 pt/10 cups water |
| 1 tsp salt (for the water) |
| 275 g/10 oz spaghetti |
| 3 carrots |
| ½ roast chicken |
| 200 g/7 oz Chinese cabbage |
| 4 sticks celery |
| 200 g/7 oz cucumber |
| 3 tbsp vinegar |
| ½ tsp salt |
| Pinch sugar |
| Pinch white pepper |
| ½ tsp soy sauce |
| 3 tbsp sesame oil |
| 2 tbsp snipped chives |

Break the spaghetti into pieces. Drop into boiling, salted water and cook for 8 minutes until 'al dente'. • Peel the carrots and cut into thin strips. Blanch for 2 minutes. Drain and leave to cool. • Skin and bone the chicken. Cut flesh into small pieces. • Cut the Chinese cabbage into thin strips. Rinse under cold running water and drain. • Wash and finely shred the celery. • Peel, wash, halve and seed the cucumber. Cut into small pieces. • Mix together the vinegar, salt, sugar, pepper and soy sauce. Fold in the oil. • Add the spaghetti, chicken and vegetables. • Sprinkle with chives.

Pasta Salad with Peppers and Sweetcorn

Inexpensive and easy

Preparation time: 1 hour
Serves 6

| 500 g/18 oz rigatoni or elbow macaroni |
| 5 litres/10 pt water |
| 2 tsp salt |
| 300 g/11 oz/2 cups frozen peas |
| 1 red pepper |
| 175 g/6 oz cooked ham |
| 275 g/10 oz/1¼ cups sweetcorn |
| 1 bunch mixed herbs (e.g. parsley, chives, basil and thyme) |
| 4 tsp vinegar |
| 1 tsp salt |
| White pepper |
| Pinch garlic powder |
| 5 tbsp oil |
| 1 bunch radishes |
| 2 hard-boiled eggs |

Cook the pasta in boiling salted water until tender, yet firm to the bite. Drain and leave to cool. Blanch the peas. Wash, seed and dice the pepper. Dice the ham. Drain the sweetcorn. Chop the herbs. Reserve 1 tbsp of mixed herbs. • Mix together the herbs, vinegar, salt, pepper, garlic powder and oil. • Slice the radishes. Peel the eggs and cut into eighths. • In a bowl mix together the pasta, peas, diced red pepper, ham, sweetcorn and half the radishes. Add the dressing. • Place the egg and remaining radish slices on top. Sprinkle with the remaining herbs.

Wholewheat Pasta and Pea Salad

Wholemeal Recipe

Preparation time: 45 minutes
Serves 4

225 g/8 oz wholewheat pasta spirals
2 litres/4 pt/8 cups water
Salt
1 green pepper
2 onions
150 g/5 oz/1 cup frozen peas
1 can tuna fish
100 g/4 oz/1 cup grated Parmesan cheese
3 tbsp sesame oil and tarragon vinegar
2 tbsp freshly chopped basil and thyme
Pinch black pepper
1 tsp paprika
1 large tomato

Drop the pasta into boiling salted water and cook for 8–10 minutes. • Wash the green pepper. Remove seeds and membranes, then slice. • Peel, halve and slice the onions. • Drain the pasta. Reserve the water. Bring to the boil. Drop in the green pepper and onions and blanch for 2 minutes. • Drop the peas into 4 tbsp of boiling water and cook for 5 minutes. • Flake the tuna fish. • Place the tuna fish liquid in a bowl. Add the grated cheese, oil, vinegar, herbs, pepper and paprika. Mix well. Place the pasta, green pepper and tuna in a bowl. Add onions and peas, slice the tomato and mix into the salad with the dressing. • Leave the salad for 5 minutes before serving.

Wholewheat Pasta and Dandelion Salad

Healthy and good

Preparation time: 1 hour
Serves 4

200 g/7 oz red or aduki kidney beans
1 bay leaf
125 g/5 oz streaky bacon
4 tbsp sunflower oil
2 litres/4 pt/8 cups water
Salt
200 g/7 oz wholewheat pasta
50 g/2 oz dandelion leaves
4 tbsp vinegar
¼ tsp freshly ground black pepper

Soak the beans in plenty of cold water for about 12 hours. • The next day, drain the beans then add to a pan of fresh water and bring to the boil. Add the bay leaf and cook rapidly for 35–40 minutes until tender. Drain well. Dice the bacon and fry in a saucepan until crisp. • Drop the pasta into boiling, salted water and cook for 10 minutes, until 'al dente'. Rinse and drain well. • Wash and finely chop the dandelion leaves. • In a bowl, mix together the pasta, dandelion leaves, bacon, vinegar, salt and pepper. • Leave to cool. • Add extra vinegar, salt and pepper to taste before serving.

Pasta and Broccoli Salad

Easy and inexpensive

Preparation time: 45 minutes
Serves 4

2 litres/4 pt/8 cups water
Salt
225 g/8 oz broccoli
150 g/5 oz spaghetti
1 courgette (zucchini)
2 tomatoes
2 hard-boiled eggs
50 g/2 oz/½ cup walnuts
100 ml/4 fl oz/½ cup single (light) cream
1 tbsp lemon juice
Pinch mixed spice
Pinch white pepper
1 tbsp snipped chives

Trim and rinse the broccoli. Cut into 2.5 cm/1 in pieces. • Drop the pasta and broccoli into boiling, salted water and cook for 10 minutes until 'al dente'. • Trim and wash the courgette (zucchini) and tomatoes and cut into pieces. • Peel the eggs and chop finely. Chop the walnuts. • In a bowl, mix together pasta, vegetables, tomatoes, eggs and nuts. Add the cream, lemon juice, salt and pinch of mixed spices and pepper. Add extra chives. • Leave the salad for 5 minutes before serving. Add extra lemon juice, salt and pepper to taste.

Pasta and Bacon Salad

Quick and easy to prepare

Preparation time: 25 minutes
Serves 4

2.5 litres/5 pt/10 cups water
Salt
250 g/9 oz wholewheat pasta (pasta spirals or rigatoni)
1 small bulb of chicory
1 onion
1 bunch chives
200 g/7 oz lean streaky bacon, thinly sliced
1 tsp oil
2–4 tbsp vinegar
Pinch cayenne pepper

Drop the pasta into boiling salted water and cook for 8–10 minutes until 'al dente'. Rinse and drain. • Clean, wash and dry the chicory and cut into thin strips. Peel and dice the onion. Wash and chop the chives. • Fry the bacon in a pan until crisp and drain on a paper towel. • Fry the onion in the oil in a pan until transparent. Remove from heat. Add the vinegar and cayenne pepper. • In a bowl, mix together the pasta, chicory, chives and the warm marinade. • Sprinkle the bacon on top. Serve immediately.

Capellini Salad

Quick and easy to prepare

Preparation time: 30 minutes
Serves 4

225 g/8 oz capellini (very thin spaghetti)
2.5 litres/5 pt/10 cups water
Salt
1 tsp oil
250 g/9 oz broccoli
1 litre/2 pt/4 cups water
2 tbsp lemon juice
Pinch nutmeg
150 g/5 oz Feta cheese
6 tbsp olive oil
1 garlic clove
4 tbsp vinegar

Drop the spaghetti into boiling, salted water with the oil and cook for 6–8 minutes until tender. Rinse and drain. • Trim and rinse the broccoli. Cut into small pieces. • Drop the broccoli into boiling, salted water and blanch for 2 minutes. Drain and sprinkle with nutmeg. • Dice the Feta. • Peel and finely chop the garlic and fry in a little oil in a pan for half a minute. Add the vinegar and remaining oil. • In a bowl, mix together all the ingredients. Serve warm.

Pasta Shells with Cream and Herbs

Pretty and tasty

Preparation time: 1 hour
Serves 4

225 g/8 oz pasta shells
2 litres/4 pt/8 cups water
Salt
500 g/18 oz red peppers
200 g/7 oz can tuna fish
2 small onions
5 hard-boiled eggs
2 tbsp oil
2 tbsp dill, chervil, parsley
1 garlic clove
1 tbsp mustard
4 tbsp yogurt
Pinch salt and white pepper
100 g/4 oz/¾ cup stoned green olives

Drop the pasta into boiling, salted water and cook for approximately 8 minutes until tender. Rinse and drain. • Wash the red peppers, remove seeds and membranes, then cut into slices. • Drain and flake the tuna fish. Peel the onions and cut into rings. Halve the eggs. • Take out the egg yolks and mix together with the oil. • Wash, dry and chop the herbs and garlic. • In a bowl mix together the herbs, garlic, mustard, yogurt and egg yolks. Add salt and pepper to taste. • Mix this together with the dressing, pasta, peppers, onion rings, tuna fish and olives. • Leave for 2 hours in a cool place.

Tagliatelle Verde Salad

Lengthy cooking time

Preparation time: 1 hour
Serves 4

200 g/7 oz tagliatelle verde
2 litres/4 pt/8 cups water
Salt
250 g/9 oz courgettes (zucchini)
500 g/18 oz asparagus
8 tbsp olive oil
Pinch each salt and freshly ground black pepper
75 g/3 oz streaky bacon
3 spring onions
1 garlic clove
4 tbsp vinegar
1 tbsp capers
3 tbsp chopped fresh parsley
1 tbsp chopped fresh basil
Pinch sugar
1 tbsp grated Parmesan cheese

Drop the pasta into boiling, salted water and cook until 'al dente'. Rinse and drain. • Top and tail the courgettes (zucchini), rinse and dry. Slice thinly in diagonal slices. • Wash the asparagus. Remove woody parts and scales, then cut into 2 cm/¾ in lengths. • Fry the courgettes (zucchini) in 2 tbsp oil for 5 minutes. Add pinch of salt and pepper. • Leave to cool. • Drop the asparagus into salted water and cook for 10–15 minutes. Drain well. • Dice the bacon and fry in 1 tbsp oil. Cut the onions into rings. • Peel and crush the garlic and mix together with vinegar, remaining salt, pepper, capers, parsley, basil, sugar and Parmesan cheese. Add the remaining oil, vegetables, pasta and bacon. • Leave for one hour before serving.

Pasta Salad with Spring Vegetables

Inexpensive and healty

Preparation time: 45 minutes
Serves 4–6

4 litres/8 pt water
Salt
400 g/14 oz pasta spirals
1 small cucumber
1 green pepper
4 tomatoes
1 kohlrabi
250 g/9 oz cooked spicy sausage
4 tbsp vinegar
Pinch each white pepper and curry powder
1 small onion
1 garlic clove
4 tbsp oil
½ bunch chives and parsley
1 bunch watercress

Drop the pasta into boiling, salted water and cook until 'al dente'. Rinse and drain. • Peel and slice the cucumber. • Wash the peppers. Remove seeds and membranes then slice. • Wash and dry tomatoes, then cut into eighths. • Trim, wash and peel kohlrabi and cut into thin strips. Skin and dice the sausage. • Mix together the vinegar, a good pinch of salt, pepper and curry powder. • Peel and grate the onion and peel and crush the garlic and add to the dressing with the oil. • Mix all the remaining ingredients together and fold into the dressing. • Toss well. • Sprinkle the chopped herbs on top. • Use the watercress as garnish.

Vegetarian Pasta Salad

A good side dish

Preparation time: 40 minutes
Serves 4–6

3 litres/6 pt/12 cups water
Salt
350 g/12 oz tagliatelle verde
2 red peppers
2 shallots
½ bunch parsley
1 bunch chives
150 g/5 oz Gorgonzola cheese
3 tbsp vinegar
150 ml/5 fl oz/⅔ cup soured cream
Freshly ground black pepper
1 hard-boiled egg

Drop the pasta into boiling, salted water and cook for 8 minutes until 'al dente'. • Halve the peppers, remove the seeds and core, wash and dry. Cut into strips. • Peel and chop the shallots. • Wash, dry and chop the parsley and chives. • Crumble the Gorgonzola and mix together with vinegar, soured cream, salt, pepper, shallots and herbs. • Reserve 1 tbsp of chives for the garnish. • Peel and chop the egg. • Mix together the pasta and red peppers. Add the cheese sauce. • Garnish with egg and chives before serving.

Pasta Salad with Green Beans

Quick and easy

Preparation time: 40 minutes
Serves 4–6

3 litres/6 pt/12 cups water
Salt
350 g/12 oz pasta quills (penne)
250 g/9 oz green beans
100 g/4 oz cooked sausage
10 green stuffed olives
1 bunch parsley
1 onion
2 tbsp mayonnaise
200 g/7 oz/¾ cup soured cream
2 tbsp vinegar
Freshly ground black pepper

Drop the pasta into boiling, salted water and cook for 8-9 minutes until tender. • Top and tail the beans. Leave small beans whole, cut others into 2.5 cm/1 in pieces. Boil in salted water for 15 minutes. Drain well. Leave to cool. Reserve 3 tbsp of the cooking liquid. • Slice the sausage and the olives finely. • Wash and dry the parsley. Chop finely. Reserve one stem for the garnish. • Peel and chop the onion finely. Mix together with the mayonnaise, soured cream, vinegar, remaining cooking liquid and chopped parsley. • Mix together the pasta, beans, sausage, and the olives. Add to the dressing. Toss well. Season with salt and pepper to taste.

Pasta Salad with Oranges

Easy and healthy

Preparation time: 40 minutes
Serves 4

250 g/9 oz pasta bows
2.5 litres/5 pt/10 cups water
Salt
1 cucumber
2 onions
2 oranges
1 red apple
3 tbsp lemon juice
150 g/5 oz set yogurt
200 g/7 oz/¾ cup soured cream
1 tbsp mayonnaise
3 tbsp orange juice
Sugar and freshly milled white pepper

Drop the pasta into boiling, salted water and cook for 8 minutes until 'al dente'. Peel and slice the cucumber. Peel and cut the onions into thin rings. • Peel the oranges, cut into segments, discarding pips and membrane. • Peel, core and slice the apple. Sprinkle with lemon juice. • In a bowl, mix together the yogurt, soured cream, mayonnaise, orange juice, salt, sugar and pepper. • Add the pasta, cucumber, onions, oranges and apple. Toss well.

Pasta Salad with Prawns

An impressive side dish

Preparation time: 40 minutes
Serves 4

2.5 litres/5 pt/10 cups water
Salt
275 g/10 oz rigatoni
225 g/8 oz/1⅓ cups prawns
4 tbsp lemon juice
1 honeydew melon
1 avocado
200 g/7 oz celery
1 bunch dill
2 tbsp mayonnaise
150 g/5 oz/⅔ cup set yogurt
3 tbsp single (light) cream
2 tbsp brandy
White pepper and cayenne pepper

Drop the pasta into boiling, salted water and cook for 8 minutes until 'al dente'. • Rinse and drain the prawns. Sprinkle with 2 tbsp lemon juice. • Peel and seed the melon and scoop into balls. • Cut the avocado in half. Take out the stone and cut into slices. Sprinkle with the remaining lemon juice. • Scrub the celery, string it, cut into slices. • Wash, dry and chop the dill, reserving a few sprigs for garnish. • Mix together the mayonnaise, yogurt, cream, brandy, pepper and cayenne. Add the dill, pasta, prawns, melon, avocado and celery. Toss well. • Garnish with dill before serving.

Pasta Salad with Mussels

Impressive

Preparation time: 1 hour
Serves 4

2 kg/4½ lb mussels
2 garlic cloves
1 large tomato
1 bunch basil or 1 tsp dried basil
8 tbsp olive oil
6 peppercorns
Pinch sugar
125 ml/4 fl oz/½ cup white wine
250 g/9 oz pasta shells
2.5 litres/5 pt/10 cups water
Salt
1 green pepper
1 bunch chopped parsley
4 tbsp vinegar
Cayenne pepper

Brush the mussels clean under cold running water. Do not use mussels with open shells. • Peel and chop the garlic. Wash and dice the tomato. Chop the basil leaves. • Fry the garlic with 2 tbsp oil in a saucepan. Add the tomato, half the basil, peppercorns, sugar and wine. • Add a little water and the mussels. Cover and cook for 5 minutes on high heat. • Unopened shells must be thrown away. Reserve the cooking liquid. • Shell the mussels. • Drop the pasta into boiling, salted water and cook for 8 minutes until 'al dente'. Rinse and drain. • Chop the green pepper. • Mix the cooking liquid from the mussels, vinegar and oil together and add all the herbs. Season with salt and cayenne pepper. Add the pasta, peppers and mussels.

Noodle Salad with Cooked Beef

Easy and quick to prepare

Preparation time: 30 minutes
Serves 4

3 litres/6 pt/12 cups water
Salt
350 g/12 oz Chinese egg noodles
250 g/9 oz bean sprouts
250 g/9 oz cooked beef
2 bunches radishes
4 spring onions
5 tbsp oil
½ tsp salt
3 tbsp vinegar
Pinch white pepper
2 tbsp soy sauce
1 tbsp sugar

Drop the noodles into boiling, salted water and cook for 6-8 minutes until tender. Rinse and drain. • Place the bean sprouts in boiling water for just a few seconds. • Drain and rinse under cold running water. • Cut the beef into small cubes. Clean, wash and slice the radishes. Wash spring onions under lukewarm water and slice into thin strips. • Mix the noodles with 2 tbsp oil. • Divide the noodles in four portions and place into four serving dishes. • Mix the remaining oil with the beef and bean sprouts and add to the noodles. • Sprinkle the radishes and spring onions on top. Blend together the vinegar, pepper, soy sauce and sugar and serve with the salad as a dressing.

Chinese White Noodle Salad with Crabmeat

Speciality from China

Preparation time: 1 hour
Serves 4

2 litres/4 pt/8 cups water
200 g/7 oz Chinese white noodles
8 black Chinese dried mushrooms (Mu Err)
400 g/14 oz crabmeat
4 spring onions
1 small can water chestnuts
1 small can bamboo shoots
1 tsp salt
2 tbsp soy sauce and sweet and sour sauce
Few drops hot chilli sauce
8 tbsp oil
3 tbsp lemon juice

Place 175 g/6 oz noodles and the same of the mushrooms in two separate bowls. • Pour boiling water over and soak for 30 minutes. • Break the crabmeat into small pieces. • Wash, dry and slice the spring onions into strips. • Rinse, drain and slice the chestnuts and bamboo shoots into thin strips. • Drain the mushrooms and cut into strips. • Drain the pasta and place in a bowl together with the chopped ingredients, salt, soy sauce, sweet and sour sauce, chilli sauce and 3 tbsp oil. Mix well together. • Heat the remaining oil in a saucepan and fry the remaining pasta until soft. • Dry on paper towel and sprinkle over the salad. • Pour the lemon juice on top.

Index